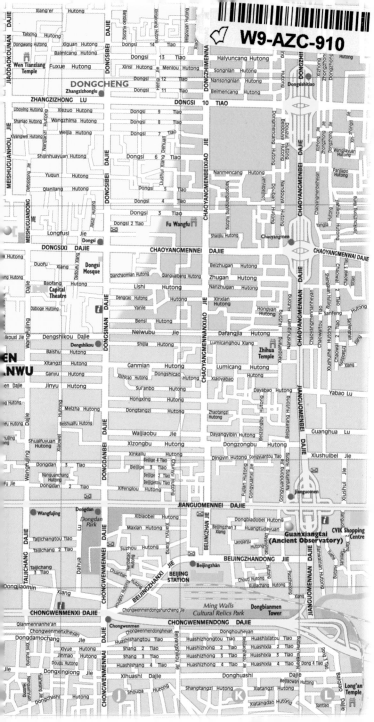

# Fodor's

# Beijing's
## 25 Best

by Sean Sheehan

Fodor's Travel Publications
New York • Toronto
London • Sydney • Auckland
www.fodors.com

# How to Use This Book

## KEY TO SYMBOLS

✚ Map reference to the accompanying fold-out map

✉ Address

☎ Telephone number

🕐 Opening/closing times

🍴 Restaurant or café

🚆 Nearest rail station

Ⓜ Nearest subway (Metro) station

🚌 Nearest bus route

⛴ Nearest riverboat or ferry stop

♿ Facilities for visitors with disabilities

❓ Other practical information

▷ Further information

ℹ Tourist information

✋ Admission charges: Expensive (over 50 yuan), Moderate (20–50 yuan), and Inexpensive (20 yuan or less)

★ Major Sight     ★ Minor Sight

👣 Walks     🚍 Excursions

🛍 Shops

🎭 Entertainment and Nightlife

🍽 Restaurants

### This guide is divided into four sections
• Essential Beijing: An introduction to the city and tips on making the most of your stay.
• Beijing by Area: We've broken the city into five areas, and recommended the best sights, shops, entertainment venues, nightlife and restaurants in each one. Suggested walks help you to explore on foot.
• Where to Stay: The best hotels, whether you're looking for luxury, budget or something in between.
• Need to Know: The info you need to make your trip run smoothly, including getting about by public transport, weather tips, emergency phone numbers and useful websites.

**Navigation** In the Beijing by Area chapter, we've given each area its own color, which is also used on the locator maps throughout the book and the map on the inside front cover.

**Maps** The fold-out map accompanying this book is a comprehensive street plan of Beijing. The grid on this fold-out map is the same as the grid on the locator maps within the book. We've given grid references within the book for each sight and listing.

# Contents

CONTENTS

# Introducing Beijing

China's capital is in the midst of a frenzy of construction—and destruction—as it prepares for the summer 2008 Olympic Games. Even once this deadline has gone, there's no sign that the city will halt its headlong rush to change and modernize.

Old neighborhoods are vanishing and high-rise apartments and business centers are springing up to take their place. But new parks are also appearing, and big-ticket infrastructure improvements to everything from the metro system to the sewage system are combining to make life in this burgeoning megalopolis more attractive.

As China's economy has continued to expand, Beijing has flourished too. This vast nation's showcase to the world looks forward confidently to more of the same and to polishing up its freshly minted role as a world capital. There's a buzz to Beijing nowadays, a feeling that anything is possible. Restaurants, bars and at least some of the many new shopping malls are thriving. Coffeehouses with Western prices are crowded with locals and the chefs in the swankiest restaurants are first-rate.

With attractions such as the Forbidden City, Tian'anmen Square, the Summer Palace and the Temple of Heaven, to name just a few (even if the most stellar), there was never any shortage of world-class places to see. Now that these have been joined by booming shopping, dining and nightlife scenes, foreign tourists are able to experience whole new dimensions to their visit to the city.

Much tranquillity has been lost along the way, and you need to scramble to catch some of the most atmospheric parts of the old city before they bite the dust. In compensation, there's an energy and self-confidence about Beijing, a sense of being on the cusp of something new and grand that is well worth experiencing.

# Facts + Figures

- At least 1 in 100 Chinese live in Beijing, which has an official population of more than 12 million.
- Beijing's Dongzhimen railway station can hold up to 14,000 people (and very often does).
- The city has six ring roads.

## GOING GREEN

It might not do much for the smog, but Beijing is in the process of getting something of a green makeover, aimed at giving it 960 parks and public gardens by the time of the 2008 Olympics, up from a mere 160 such spaces in 2002. In addition, despite a rapidly growing number of private cars, 9 million Beijingers cycle every day.

## AIR ASSAULT

Development has in some respects proved a mixed blessing, or at any rate has its downside. On most days a thick smog hangs low over the city, especially in winter. No longer can you see the ring of forest-clad mountains surrounding the city, as you do in old photographs.

## SMOKING

There are few, if any, restrictions on smoking in bars, cafés or restaurants. Even where there are designated nonsmoking areas, these are often honored more in the breach than the observance. Asking for a nonsmoking table in a restaurant will often be met by a bemused stare.

# A Short Stay in Beijing

## DAY 1

**Morning** Start out with an early breakfast at the **Beijing Raffles Hotel** (▷ 112), which should set you up nicely for a long morning. From there, walk west along Dongchang'an Jie to the **Tian'anmen Gate** (▷ 52–53) to enter the **Forbidden City** (Palace Museum, ▷ 24–25).

**Mid-morning** Relax over a pot of Chinese tea at one of the teahouses inside the Forbidden City. Touring the Forbidden City is really an activity for an entire day (at least), but if you are to see other parts of the city, a morning will suffice. Be sure to visit the buildings along the central axis (▷ 26–31)—the **Hall of Middle Harmony**, **Hall of Preserving Harmony** and **Hall of Supreme Harmony**, and the **Imperial Garden** (▷ 32–33).

**Lunch** If a slice of pizza would serve as a quick and not too heavy lunch, try **Hutong Pizza** (▷ 89), in its atmospheric old *hutong* house.

**Afternoon** Explore part of the old *hutongs* of the Back Lakes district north of Beihai Park, going out as far as the **Bell and Drum Towers** (▷ 84) if you have the energy.

**Mid-afternoon** Stroll through **Beihai Park** (▷ 80–81) and visit the **White Dagoba** on Jade Island at the heart of the park's lake. You can avoid doing too much walking by taking a boat tour or renting a row boat.

**Dinner** Dine on delicate Vietnamese cuisine—at a patio table if the weather is fine—at the lakefront restaurant **Nuage** (▷ 90).

**Evening** For a musical evening you could choose either classical Chinese music at the **Beijing Concert Hall** (▷ 88) or jazz at the **East Shore Live Jazz Café** (▷ 88).

## DAY 2

**Morning** After breakfast at your hotel, stroll south through emblematic **Tian'anmen Square** (▷ 52–53), where you can visit the **Chairman Mao Memorial Hall** (▷ 44) if you have the stomach for perusing the late "Great Helmsman's" mummified corpse, or visit instead the **National Museum of China** (▷ 45).

**Mid-morning** From the **Qianmen Gate** (▷ 46–47), a walk (or taxi ride) south of about 1 mile (1.6km) brings you to the Temple of Heaven Park to visit the **Temple of Heaven** (▷ 50–51) and other temples and altars at this impressive imperial complex.

**Lunch** Have a light but refined Indian vegetarian lunch at **The Taj Pavilion** (▷ 62).

**Afternoon** A bus trip to the **Summer Palace** (▷ 100–101) on the north-western edge of the city will occupy the whole afternoon, but it's worth it to view this fabulous imperial garden and its lakes, temples and extravagant pavilions.

**Mid-afternoon** Stop for refreshment at one of the snack bars or tea-houses at the Palace, then take a boat trip on the main lake.

**Dinner** Back in town, for a taste of the very best of Beijing's own specialty, Peking roast duck, go to **Quanjude Kaoyadian** (▷ 62).

**Evening** If you are up for a burst of Chinese opera, there's no better place than the **Liyuan Theater** (▷ 60), but if you would prefer to hang out with expats in a pub, try **Durty Nellie's** (▷ 74) instead.

# Top 25

TOP 25

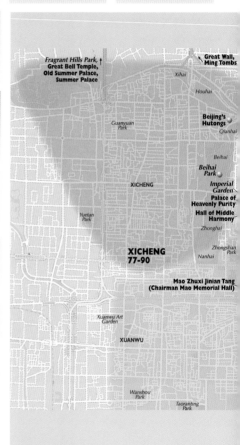

Fragrant Hills Park,
Great Bell Temple,
Old Summer Palace,
Summer Palace

Great Wall,
Ming Tombs

Xihai

Houhai

Guanyuan
Park

Beijing's
Hutongs

Qianhai

Beihai

Beihai
Park

Imperial
Garden
Palace of
Heavenly Purity

XICHENG

Yuetan
Park

Hall of Middle
Harmony

Zhonghai

XICHENG
77–90

Zhongshan
Park

Nanhai

Mao Zhuxi Jinian Tang
(Chairman Mao Memorial Hall)

Xuanwu Art
Garden

XUANWU

Wanshou
Park

Taoranting
Park

These pages are a quick guide to the Top 25, which are described in more detail later. Here they are listed alphabetically, and the tinted background shows which area they are in.

**Chairman Mao Memorial Hall ▷ 44**
Chairman Mao lies in state in a hall built by volunteers.

**Forbidden City (Palace Museum) ▷ 24–25** The former heart of the Chinese empire.

**Fragrant Hills Park ▷ 94** A scenic escape from the city at all seasons, with interesting temples.

**Great Bell Temple ▷ 95**
The 15th-century Yongle Bell is housed here.

**The Great Wall ▷ 96–97** The archetypal symbol of China, it took 2,000 years to build.

**Hall of Middle Harmony ▷ 26–27** The emperor's robing room.

**Hall of Preserving Harmony ▷ 28–29** Magnificent hall known for its "Dragon Walk."

**Hall of Supreme Harmony ▷ 30–31** The largest timber structure in China was used for major ceremonies.

**Imperial Garden ▷ 32–33** The Forbidden City's palace garden is a refreshing place for a rest.

**Jingshan Park ▷ 66** Take a break from the history in Beijing's vast "green lung."

**Lama Temple ▷ 68–69** The largest statue of the Buddha carved from a single block of wood resides in this former palace.

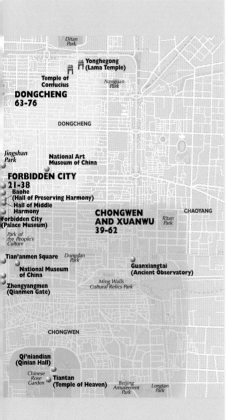

Ditan Park

Yonghegong (Lama Temple)

Temple of Confucius

Nanguan Park

**DONGCHENG 63–76**

DONGCHENG

Jingshan Park

National Art Museum of China

**FORBIDDEN CITY 21–38**
Baohe (Hall of Preserving Harmony)
Hall of Middle Harmony
Forbidden City (Palace Museum)

**CHONGWEN AND XUANWU 39–62**

Ritan Park

CHAOYANG

Park of the People's Culture

Tian'anmen Square

Dongdan Park

National Museum of China

Guanxiangtai (Ancient Observatory)

Zhengyangmen (Qianmen Gate)

Ming Walls Cultural Relics Park

CHONGWEN

Qi'niandian (Qinian Hall)

Chinese Rose Garden

Tiantan (Temple of Heaven)

Beijing Amusement Park

Longtan Park

**National Art Museum of China ▷ 67** A striking contemporary building with paintings of Chinese life.

**Ming Tombs ▷ 98–99** A monumental approach leads to the resting place of 13 Ming emperors.

◀ ◀ ◀

# Shopping

From five pairs of socks for a little more than a US dollar to Chinese calligraphy sets, from real antiques to genuine fakes, designer items to knockoffs, you can find it all in Beijing stores, malls and markets—and don't ignore street-corner hawkers out of hand.

## Clothing

Clothes and shoes no longer come in small sizes only. A fattened-up populace—another product of Beijing's rising affluence—means that even normal to larger Westerners can find Chinese clothing that fits off the peg. Larger shoes, tops and trousers are now widely available in both the Silk Market and stores. Moreover, service is increasingly easy to find. Nowadays, shopkeepers will hold up a curtain for you to change behind, or show you to the back room to try clothes on. Many stores have end-of-season sales (March for winter goods and August for summer) that can yield steep mark-downs on high-end fashions.

## Markets

No matter where you shop in Beijing, knowing your product and buying with caution are key. Check out purportedly genuine Chinese antiques thoroughly, as fakes abound. Even with that caution, the markets—from Hongqiao market, which sells everything from pearls to antiques, to the Silk Market, which sells everything from silk (obviously) to leather boots—are fun to visit even if you're not planning to buy

### CLOISONNÉ

Cloisonné is an attractive, colorful enamel finish applied to many types of decorative ware such as lamps, vases, incense burners, tea sets, tables and silver-based items. It is produced by welding flattened wire on to a copper backing to form an outline. Enamel of different colors is then used to fill the outlined spaces with a range of rich shades. An art dating back to the Ming dynasty (1368–1644), it remains popular today.

*Chinese clover flower tea; calligraphy brushes; silk jackets; silk sandals (top to bottom)*

anything. Aside from the classic Chairman Mao buttons, curios to look out for include place-mats and napkin sets with chopsticks, hand-painted scrolls, name chops and mahjong sets.

### Haggling

Some, although not all, vendors can be aggressive, screaming out in English, Spanish, Japanese and Russian to get your attention. But once you're bargaining, humor can rule the day. Beware, of course, the humor is sometimes at your expense: They'll laugh as they try to sell you something that clearly doesn't fit or is clearly not made of "pure silk." "Buyer beware" remains the advice in the markets.

### The Street Scene

But at other times the traders' humor is just about enjoying life while working 12- and 14-hour days, seven days a week. In winter, cigarette vendors stick Marlboros in carrot-nosed snowmen. In the summer, you may have to interrupt impromptu soccer and hackey-sack games between stand vendors if you want to get their attention. Go with a sense of adventure and you're sure to enjoy the day. If street markets are exotic pieces of old China doing their best to survive and prosper, the glittering malls that have sprung up and continue to spring up in the city's commercial districts are more familiar.

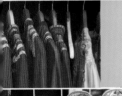

*Painted tea mugs (top); Yings Fashion Studio in the Chaoyang District (middle)*

### CHOPS

Personalized stamps—name chops—have been used for thousands of years in China and, despite mass literacy, are still commonly used. In a number of official situations, where the West would demand a signature, the Chinese stamp a document with their personal chop. The chops are made from a variety of materials—marble, jade, wood and even plastic—and better arts and crafts stores stock a good selection. It is easy to have your name put on one in Chinese characters or in your own language. When making a purchase, be sure to get an ink pad and ink—red is the traditional color.

# Shopping by Theme

Whether you're looking for a department store, a quirky boutique, or something in between, you'll find it all in Beijing. On this page shops are listed by theme. For a more detailed write-up, see the individual listings in Beijing by Area.

# Beijing by Night

Kick off your night with Peking duck, a Thai curry or Italian pasta in a local restaurant. Dining rooms in many hotels serve authentic food, but, especially for Northern Chinese cuisine, chances are that you can get the same meal for a fraction of the price across the street. And while it's a good idea to polish your chopstick skills before you come to China, most upscale restaurants can provide a knife and fork if you need them.

### Bar Hopping
The Sanlitun area is still the hottest in town. From Durty Nellie's (with chatty waitresses and on-tap Guinness) to The Tree (which serves up tasty pizza and salads washed down with Belgian beers), you can bar hop without ever getting a taxi. Throughout town, any place where you see "KTV"—for Karaoke TV—is fun to visit for the kitsch factor. But be warned: Waitresses are pushy, drinks are expensive and the bars can be tacky, although they attract a local clientele, too.

### Ode to Opera
No trip to Beijing is complete without a night at the opera. Beijing Opera is all-around theater: You get acting, acrobatics, martial arts, dance, costumes, makeup and music. The music may be an acquired taste (the word "screeching" might come to a first-timer's mind) but it's certainly an experience.

*Beijing bar hopping (above). Head to the Sanlitun area for great nightlife*

| LISTINGS |
| --- |

Several English-language magazines provide visitors and expatriates with easily accessible information about what's on, and all of them have their own websites. The monthly magazines *Beijing This Month* and *That's Beijing* cover events, listings, reviews and features about life in the city, and more; their associated websites are www.btmbeijing.com and www.thatsbj.com. Then, there's the bi-weekly *City Weekend* magazine's Beijing edition, online at www.cityweekend.com.cn/beijing.

# Eating Out

In Beijing you can look forward to sampling the cuisine of virtually every Chinese region, as well as the culinary traditions of the imperial court. Eating out still represents great value for money.

## Where to Eat
While restaurants are scattered widely across the capital, if you head for Houhai, Sanlitun or Nanluogu Xiang, you'll find plenty of lively bars and cafés serving Western and Chinese food in less formal surroundings.

## Restaurants
When you arrive at a restaurant you will be greeted at the door with a *huanying* ("welcome") before being shown to your table. Tea will be served while you are consulting the menu. In China it is customary to order dishes to share, so choose a number of items from different parts of the menu. Serve yourself from the communal dish using your chopsticks and eat from the small plate in front of you—the bowl is for rice or soup.

## Payment
Although many restaurants will accept credit cards, this is still a cash economy, so don't count on it. A service charge of 10 percent will be included in the bill. This does not go to the wait staff, so if the service has been good, you may like to leave a few yuan as a tip.

### WHEN TO EAT
Breakfast is taken early in China—most restaurants are open by 7.30am. The traditional breakfast dish is *congee* (rice porridge). Street food is popular at this time of day, especially steamed buns or the elongated, crispy fried doughnuts known in Beijing as *youtiao*. By around 11am the Chinese will be thinking about lunch, usually a simple affair of one or two courses. Dinner, the main meal of the day can begin as early as 5pm. If you arrive in a restaurant much after 8pm the waitresses will be scowling at you or sweeping around your feet while you eat.

*An evening meal in a Beijing restaurant; a tea seller; edible locusts; a noodle dish (top to bottom)*

# Restaurants by Cuisine

There are restaurants to suit all tastes and budgets in Beijing. On this page they are listed by cuisine. For a more detailed description of each restaurant, see Beijing by Area.

## ASIAN

Asian Star (▷ 76)
Café Sambal (▷ 89)
Hatsune (▷ 61)
Nuage (▷ 90)
Serve The People (▷ 76)
The Taj Pavilion (▷ 62)
The Tandoor (▷ 76)

## BEIJING

Bianyifang Roast Duck
  Restaurant (▷ 61)
King Roast Duck (▷ 62)
Li Jia Cai Imperial
  Restaurant (▷ 89)
Mei Fu (▷ 90)
Quanjude Kaoyadian
  (▷ 62)
Red Capital (▷ 62)
Yueming Lou (▷ 90)

## CANTONESE

Beijing Ah Yat Abalone
  Restaurant (▷ 61)

## CHINESE (MIXED)

Afunti (▷ 76)
Ding Tai Zhen (▷ 76)
Fangshan (▷ 89)
Food St. (▷ 89)
Golden Palace (▷ 89)
Kaorou Ji (▷ 89)
The Middle 8th Restaurant
  (▷ 76)

## EUROPEAN

Bleu Marine (▷ 61)
Le Café Igosso (▷ 61)
Danieli's (▷ 61)
Justine's (▷ 62)
Moscow (▷ 90)

## INTERNATIONAL

Hutong Pizza (▷ 89)
Mexican Wave (▷ 62)
Pass By Bar (▷ 76)
Steak and Eggs (▷ 62)

## SICHUAN

Ba Guo Bu Yi (▷ 76)
Neng Ren Ju (▷ 90)
Sichuan Restaurant (▷ 90)

## VEGETARIAN

Gongdelin (▷ 61)

# If You Like...

However you'd like to spend your time in Beijing, these top suggestions should help you tailor your ideal visit. Each sight or listing has a fuller write-up in Beijing by Area.

## INTERNATIONAL SHOPPING

**Foreign Languages Bookstore** (▷ 73): An important resource for anyone whose Chinese ranges from rusty to nonexistent.
**China World Shopping Mall** (▷ 58): One of the new high temples to consumerism that has brought the term "lifestyle" to the capital.
**Kerry Centre** (▷ 58): A veritable melting-pot of international products gathered under one roof.
**Carrefour** (▷ 87): Stocks Western eatables and other products.

## LOCAL CUISINE

**Try the Cantonese cuisine** for discerning Beijingese and visitors at Beijing Ah Yat Abalone Restaurant (▷ 61).
**Enjoy dining** at Quanjude (▷ 62): The state of the art when it comes to roast Beijing duck.
**Delight in** the food and entertainment from China's Muslim Uighur community at Afunti (▷ 76).
**Sample** the Middle 8th Restaurant's (▷ 76) sophisticated, authentic Yunnan cuisine.

*Books for sale (above) in the Foreign Languages Bookstore; local cuisine (below)*

## HOT AND COOL

**Soak up the relaxed vibe** at CD Café Jazz Club (▷ 74): it has a broad musical range.
**Join the expats** at Durty Nellie's (▷ 74), a popular Irish/Continental bar.
**Listen to** sophisticated jazz in a laid-back lakeside setting at East Shore Live Jazz Café (▷ 88).
**Head to** 13 Club (▷ 88): A grungy setting for local bands and beer.

*There are several jazz venues in Beijing (right)*

*Spa pampering; kite-flying on Tian'anmen Square (below)*

## A PAMPERED LIFESTYLE

**Indulge yourself** at the Peninsula Beijing (▷112), a most luxurious hotel.

**Imagine** what it was like for the emperor to be honored by his court in the Hall of Supreme Harmony (▷30–31).

**Kick back** in comfortable chairs over homemade Italian pasta at Danieli's (▷61).

**Finish** a hard day's sightseeing with a Finnish sauna at the Radisson SAS hotel (▷112).

## ACTIVITIES FOR KIDS

**Fly a kite** on Tian'anmen Square (▷52–53).

**Experience** rides, slides, boats and more at Beijing Amusement Park (▷54) in Longtan Lake Park.

**Rent a row boat** in scenic Beihai Park (▷80–81) to get a well-earned break from walking.

**Get close** to the native inhabitants of the sea, among them sharks, at Beijing Aquarium (▷84).

## THE SCENT OF SANCTITY

*A brightly-colored fish at Beijing Aquarium (above)*

**Smell the flowers** at Fayuan Temple (▷54), a Buddhist temple dating back to the Tang dynasty.

**Seek serenity** at White Cloud Temple (▷56), Beijing's oldest Taoist temple.

**See the Lama Temple** (▷68–69); despite being a showcase of "Chinese Tibet," this Buddhist temple has elements of authenticity.

**Enjoy peace and quiet** at the Temple of Confucius (▷70–71): The principal Confucian foundation in Beijing is a serene place.

*The Temple of Confucius (left)*

*Chinese entertainment; green Beijing (below)*

## CHINESE ENTERTAINMENT

**Visit** Zhengyici Theater (▷ 60): A 17th-century teahouse and venue for Chinese opera.
**Go to** Tian Qiao Acrobatics Theater (▷ 60), the main in-town venue for Beijing's highly regarded acrobatic troupe.
**Experience a breath of fresh air** for Chinese theater at the Experimental Theater for Modern Drama (▷ 74).

## GREEN SPACES

**Relax** in the Imperial Garden (▷ 32–33), the emperors' private retreat in the Forbidden City.
**Escape from** the capital's polluted air to fresh mountain breezes at Fragrant Hills Park (▷ 94).
**Savor the tranquillity** at the Old Summer Palace (▷ 102), which was destroyed by invading troops, leaving behind a beautiful park.

## MAO MOMENTS

**China's late leader** continues to watch over his people from Chairman Mao Memorial Hall (▷ 44).
**Monument to the People's Heroes** (▷ 55): A granite obelisk glorifies the Communist revolution.
**Mao famously said** that anyone wishing to be a hero must first climb the Great Wall (▷ 96–97).

*Chairman Mao (above); acupuncture (below)*

## LOOKING FOR A BARGAIN

**Stay** at Jinghua Hotel (▷ panel, 109), aimed at young travelers.
**Haggle** over Mao and Revolution kitsch at Tiantan Park Market (▷ 59).
**Try** acupuncture or herbalism at the Taoist White Cloud Temple (▷ 56).
**Check out** the clothes at Ganjiakou (▷ 87).

# Beijing by Area

**FORBIDDEN CITY**

**CHONGWEN AND XUANWU**

**DONGCHENG**

**XICHENG**

**FARTHER AFIELD**

Residence of emperors and their courts for 500 years, the vast and lavish Forbidden City is open to all, affording visitors an unforgettable encounter with imperial China.

Shenwu
Gate

*Imperial
Garden*

Hall of Union

Hall of Mental
Cultivation

Palace of
Heavenly Purity

Baohe
(Hall of Preserving
Harmony)

Hall of Middle
Harmony

Nine Dragon
Screen

Taihedian
(Hall of Supreme
Harmony)

Forbidden City
(Palace Museum)

Wumen
(Meridian Gate)

Tongzi

3

4

5

6

F

G

0      250 m

0      250 yds

Tongzi

*Bronze lion (opposite); Gate of Heavenly Purity (left); bronze crane (middle); bright rooftops (right)*

# Forbidden City (Palace Museum)

**Wander off the beaten track to imagine the past: emperors and empresses, court intrigues, palaces and thrones. This was the imperial heart of Chinese civilization.**

**A perfect balance** No other complex can match the Forbidden City in its harmonious mix of monumental scale, fine detail and geometry. Between 1420 and 1911 it was the residence and court of the Ming and Qing dynasties; now it is a museum complex, formally known as the Palace Museum (Gu Gong), including major sites—official buildings, residencies, gates and gardens—that are visitor must-sees. Begin at the main entrance, the Meridian Gate (Wumen, ▷ 36), through the 33ft (10m) wall that surrounds the complex with watchtowers on all corners. The wall itself is surrounded by a moat more than 165ft (50m) across.

**Orientation** The main buildings in the Forbidden City are laid out on a north–south axis, starting from the south with the Halls of Supreme Harmony (Taihe), Middle Harmony (Zhonge) and Preserving Harmony (Baohe). The Gate of Heavenly Purity (Quianqingmen) separates these official buildings from the residential quarter, the focal points of which are the Palace of Heavenly Purity (Quianqing Palace) and the Palace of Earthly Tranquillity (Kunninggong). Behind the royal bedrooms lies the Imperial Garden.

**Elitism** Ordinary Chinese citizens were executed if they entered the complex—hence the unofficial epithet "Forbidden City."

### THE BASICS

www.dpm.org.cn

✚ G4–G5

✉ Xichang'an Jie, Dongcheng District

☎ 6513 2255

🕐 Apr–Oct daily 8.30–5; Nov–Mar daily 8.30–4.30. Last admission tickets are sold 1 hour before closing

🍴 Snack shop in the Imperial Garden

🚇 Tiananmen Xi, Tiananmen Dong

🚌 1, 4, 10, 22, 203

♿ None

💲 Moderate

❓ Taped guided tours in various languages can be rented at southern entrance and returned at northern exit

### HIGHLIGHTS

● Hall of Supreme Harmony (▷ 30–31)
● Hall of Middle Harmony (▷ 26–27)
● Palace of Heavenly Purity (▷ 34–35)

# Hall of Middle Harmony

---

## HIGHLIGHTS

● Ornamental ceiling
● Emperor's sedan chairs

## TIP

● Parts of the Forbidden City may be closed due to a massive rebuilding and refurbishment project that is not due to be completed until 2020. Should there be a particular element of the complex structure that you wish to see, it might be worth checking that it is in fact open to the public.

**Best viewed from a distance, perhaps standing on the marble terrace, the Hall of Middle Harmony is a perfect example of imperial architecture. The design demonstrates the popular use of open space to enhance buildings.**

**Imperial dressing room** Of the three main halls aligned on the north–south axis of the Forbidden City, this is the smallest. It generally functioned as an all-purpose imperial hall. Here the emperor would be decked out in his fine regalia before proceeding to whatever important ceremony or event was taking place in the Hall of Supreme Harmony (▷ 30–31). Some relatively minor court procedures, such as the inspection of seeds before planting, would take place in the Hall of Middle Harmony (also known as Zhonge Hall). This was

*Visitors climbing the steps to the Hall of Middle Harmony (far left); detail of yellow roof tiles (middle); the interior of the Hall (right); visitors outside the Hall (bottom left); the emperor's cushioned chair (bottom middle); terraced stairs leading up to the Hall of Middle Harmony and the Hall of Preserving Harmony (bottom right)*

also where the emperor held audiences with high-ranking court officials or influential foreigners, and where dress rehearsals for court rituals took place.

**A smaller scale** The Hall of Middle Harmony is not just a smaller version of the other two halls—it has its own unique features. First constructed in 1420, it was rebuilt in 1627 and the roof design is different, although it has the same overhanging eaves with decorative figures along the end of each ridge. The smaller size of this hall allows you to take in the harmonies of its proportions without being overawed by the scale. The interior has a carpeted platform and two cushioned sedan chairs that were reserved for the emperor. The interior columns are not as richly embellished as those in the other two halls, but the small squares that make up the ceiling are finely decorated.

## THE BASICS

- ⊞ G5
- ✉ Forbidden City
- 🕐 Apr–Oct daily 8.30–5; Nov–Mar daily 8.30–4.30. Last admission tickets are sold 1 hour before closing
- 🚇 Tiananmen Xi, Tiananmen Dong
- 🚌 1, 4, 10, 22, 203
- ♿ None
- 🎫 Included in admission fee to Forbidden City
- ❓ The Hall of Middle Harmony's name is also variously translated as the Hall of Complete Harmony and the Hall of Perfect Harmony

27

# Hall of Preserving Harmony

## HIGHLIGHTS

- Dragon Walk
- Marble Terrace
- Archeological finds from the site, on display inside the hall
- Archery Pavilion (to the east of the hall)

**When you see the remarkable marble Dragon Walk at the rear of this hall, the story of how it got there is a reminder of what the designers and builders of the Forbidden City achieved—all without the aid of machinery.**

**Banquets and examinations** The Hall of Preserving Harmony (Baohe Hall) is one of the Forbidden City's three great halls. Behind it, to the north, the Gate of Heavenly Purity marks the division between the official, ceremonial sector to the south and the more private residential area to the north. At first, the Hall of Preserving Harmony was reserved for the royal banquets that usually concluded major ceremonial events. Later, during the rule of Emperor Yongzheng (1723–35) in the Qing dynasty, the notoriously difficult higher-level

*The solid marble Dragon Walk (left); the painted roofs (middle); visitors viewed through the columns opposite (right); view of the Hall of Preserving Harmony from the Hall of Supreme Harmony (bottom left); the exterior of the Hall of Preserving Harmony (bottom middle); inside the hall (bottom right)*

imperial examinations were held here. Successful candidates were assured of promotion to top-rank bureaucratic positions, so the competition was intense.

**Dragon Walk** Directly behind the hall, a broad marble walkway leads down from the terrace and forms the middle of a set of steps. It is known as the Dragon Walk: A design motif depicts nine dragons flying above swirling clouds. Some 10,000 men were needed to excavate the marble; to transport the 250-ton block the 31 miles (50km) from its quarry, wells were dug along the route to provide water. This was poured along the road and in the cold winter temperatures turned into a carpet of ice. The marble block was pulled along this ice track, it is said, by up to 1,000 horses tied together.

### THE BASICS

➕ G4
✉ Forbidden City
🕐 Apr–Oct daily 8.30–5; Nov–Mar daily 8.30–4.30. Last admission tickets are sold 1 hour before closing
🚇 Tiananmen Xi, Tiananmen Dong
🚌 1, 4, 10, 22, 203
♿ None
💷 Included in admission fee to Forbidden City

# Hall of Supreme Harmony

### HIGHLIGHTS

● The ornate ceiling
● Richly decorated columns, carved with gold-foil dragons
● The Dragon Throne and the nine-dragon screen behind it

### TIP

● That word "City" isn't there for nothing. You're unlikely to get much out of a first visit of less than a half day, and a day would be better. You might also want to set aside additional days.

**Here, the court population, numbering thousands, waited in silence as the emperor ascended to his throne, then ritually kowtowed nine times, while the eunuch choir rejoiced in song.**

**The throne room** Inside the Forbidden City, beyond the Meridian Gate (▷ 36), a courtyard leads to the Gate of Supreme Harmony and a stream crossed by five marble bridges. Two imposing bronze lions stand guard, the male holding an orb in his paw and the female a cub, a symbol of power and longevity. The vast courtyard ahead is dominated by the grandest single building in the Forbidden City, the Hall of Supreme Harmony (Taihe Hall). Here the robed emperor arrived in his yellow sedan chair to preside over important court ceremonies: coronations, royal birthdays, the

*A bronze crane (far left); a huge incense burner (middle); visitors making their way to the entrance of the Hall of Supreme Harmony (right); a giant turtle incense burner (bottom left); the lavish Dragon Throne in the interior (bottom middle); detail of the Dragon Throne (bottom right)*

New Year and the winter solstice. In the marble courtyard stood the armed, personal bodyguards, ceremonially dressed in red satin suits, while members of the royal family filled the marble staircase.

**Symbolism** The Hall of Supreme Harmony stands majestically upon a three-tiered terrace, with its own small courtyard surrounded by a marble balustrade. The stairway is furnished with bronze incense burners and in the courtyard are further symbols of longevity, bronze tortoises and cranes that have a space inside for burning incense. A pile of grains on the west side of the terrace and a sundial on the east symbolize the power of justice that resided with the imperial government. Entry to the hall is prohibited, but the splendid interior may be viewed from the open doorway.

**THE BASICS**

G5
Forbidden City
Apr–Oct daily 8.30–5; Nov–Mar daily 8.30–4.30. Last admission tickets are sold 1 hour before closing
Tiananmen Xi, Tiananmen Dong
1, 4, 10, 22, 203
Included in admission fee to Forbidden City

### HIGHLIGHTS

● Rock garden
● Exhibition halls to the east of the garden
● Top of the north wall and view of Jingshan Park

### TIP

● Most visitors are justifiably weary by the time they reach the northern end of the Forbidden City, so allow time to rest in the garden. An old lodge dispenses snacks, clean toilets are available and there are some reason-abe tourist stores.

**A classic traditional Chinese garden, comprising trees and water in harmony with a rock garden and temples. Refreshments here are served in the "Lodge for the Proper Places and Cultivation of Things."**

**Supreme sanctuary** There are four gardens within the Forbidden City but this one—some 300ft by 435ft (90m by 30m)—is the largest and most impressive. The arrangement of walkways, jade benches, pavilions and ponds was laid out during the Ming dynasty and, despite the fact that there are 20 buildings dotted around the place, the overall impression is of a relaxing natural setting. The imperial family had the Summer Palace (▷ 100–101) and other rural resorts to retreat to en masse, but the Imperial Garden (Yu Hua Yuan),

*The One Thousand Autumns Pavilion (left and right); bell covered in Chinese characters (bottom left); the ornately painted ceiling of the One Thousand Autumns Pavilion (bottom middle); a dragon guarding the gateway to the Imperial Garden (bottom right)*

at the north end of the Forbidden City, was more readily available.

**Repose** The artificial rock garden, with a pleasing little temple perched on the summit, is one of the garden's most picturesque aspects, and was one of the few places from which permanent denizens of the palace, particularly the cloistered women of the imperial family, could catch a glimpse of the world beyond the walls. Large bronze elephants, with their faded gilt, contribute to an air of antiquity that is maintained by the centuries-old cypresses, which look as if they are near the end of their natural lives. Surrounding bamboo plants are readily recognized but there are also other, rarer, plants in some of the flower beds. Water is not such an important feature of this garden as in other major gardens in China, but there are two small pools.

**THE BASICS**

➕ G4
✉ Forbidden City
🕐 Apr–Oct daily 8.30–5; Nov–Mar daily 8.30–4.30. Last admission tickets are sold 1 hour before closing
🚇 Tiananmen Xi, Tiananmen Dong
🚌 1, 4, 10, 22, 203
♿ None
🎟 Included in admission fee to Forbidden City

# Palace of Heavenly Purity

## HIGHLIGHTS

● Hall of Mental Cultivation (▷ 36)
● Exhibition halls and museums of imperial treasures (east of Palace of Earthly Tranquillity)

## TIP

● Gift Shop, just inside the north gate, has a selection of art books, reproductions of Ming and Qing art and other souvenirs. The bookstore next door has the city's best selection of translated academic titles on Chinese art and archeology.

**Stories of passion and family intrigue have unfolded in this residential complex containing the private bedrooms of the emperors and empresses: In 1542 a maid nearly strangled Emperor Jiajing here.**

**Emperors at home**  Beyond the Gate of Heavenly Purity lie the more private imperial residential quarters of the Forbidden City. The Palace of Heavenly Purity (also known as Quianqing Palace), during the Ming dynasty, was reserved as the bedroom of the emperor—the empress had her own quarters in the adjacent Palace of Earthly Tranquillity. The Qing dynasty preferred a less formal arrangement. Royalty lived in other rooms east and west of the main buildings, but the formal significance of the Palace of Heavenly Purity was not lost. When a Qing emperor died, his body

*The dragon ramp leading up to the Palace of Heavenly Purity (left); intricately carved mirror reflecting the bedroom (middle); the emperor's gilded bedroom (right)*

was placed in the palace for a few days to signify he had lived a good life and had died while sleeping in his own bedroom. The successor to the throne was announced from here.

**A red face** The palace was the place for the consummation of royal marriages, where the newly married emperor would spend the first days with his wife. The last emperor, Puyi, who came to the room in 1922 on his wedding night as a young teenager, reported as follows: "The bride sat down on her bed, her head bent down. I looked around me and saw that everything was red: Red bed-curtains, red pillows, a red dress, a red skirt, red flowers and a red face…it all looked like a melted red wax candle. I did not know whether to stand or sit, decided I preferred the Hall of Mental Cultivation, and went back there."

**THE BASICS**

➕ G4

✉ Forbidden City

🕐 Apr–Oct daily 8.30–5; Nov–Mar daily 8.30–4.30. Last admission tickets are sold 1 hour before closing

🚇 Tiananmen Xi, Tiananmen Dong

🚌 1, 4, 10, 22, 203

♿ None

🎟 Included in admission fee to Forbidden City (but small extra charge for some exhibition halls)

# More to See

## HALL OF MENTAL CULTIVATION (YANGXINDIANG)

One of the many private rooms on the west side of the northern half of the Forbidden City, this hall was home to Empress Dowager Cixi and also used by the Emperor Puyi as a bedroom.
✚ G4 ✉ Xichang'an Jie, Dongcheng District ☎ 6513 2255 🕐 Apr–Oct daily 8.30–5; Nov–Mar daily 8.30–4.30. Last admission tickets are sold 1 hour before closing 🍴 Snack shop in the Imperial Garden 🚇 Tiananmen Xi, Tiananmen Dong 🍴 Moderate (included in entrance ticket to Forbidden City)

## HALL OF UNION

The Hall of Union, standing between the Palace of Heavenly Purity (▷ 34) and the Palace of Earthly Tranquillity, is the middle of the three inner halls in the residential area of the Forbidden City. During the Qing dynasty, it was used for royal birthdays and coronations. It now contains a set of imperial jade seals, a glockenspiel and an 18th-century clepsydra, a time-measuring device worked by flowing water.

✚ G4 ✉ Xichang'an Jie, Dongcheng District ☎ 6513 2255 🕐 Apr–Oct daily 8.30–5; Nov–Mar daily 8.30–4.30. Last admission tickets are sold 1 hour before closing 🍴 Snack shop in the Imperial Garden 🚇 Tiananmen Xi, Tiananmen Dong 🚫 None 🍴 Moderate (included in entrance ticket to Forbidden City)

## MERIDIAN GATE (WUMEN)

This is the largest and most important of the four entrance gates to the Forbidden City. Usually only the emperor could use the center of the five arched portals, but exceptions were made for the empress on her wedding day and for the three candidates who gained the highest marks in each year's imperial examinations, who used the gate once. From here, the emperor passed sentence on captured enemy soldiers, inspected his troops and presented the New Year's calendar to court officials. Today's U-shaped, multi-eaved gate dates back to the 17th century when it was substantially restored.
✚ G5 ✉ Xichang'an Jie, Dongcheng

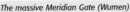

*The massive Meridian Gate (Wumen)*

District ☎ 6513 2255 🕐 Apr–Oct daily 8.30–5; Nov–Mar daily 8.30–4.30. Last admission tickets are sold 1 hour before closing 🍴 Snack shop in the Imperial Garden 🚇 Tiananmen Xi, Tiananmen Dong 🚫 None 💰 Moderate (included in entrance ticket to Forbidden City)

### NINE DRAGON SCREEN

On the east side of the outer courtyard, this wall, 98ft (30m) long and 11ft (3.5m) high and faced with colored glazed tiles, dates from the 1770s and bears striking images of dragons. The mythical creatures have five claws, which makes them symbols of the emperor. They are portrayed cavorting with pearls above a wave-tossed sea. The screen was built for the Qianlong emperor as a defence against evil spirits—and more practically, as a protection against prying eyes. It stands at the heart of a less-visited part of the Forbidden City, an area of "minor" palaces that were residences for empresses and concubines.

✚ G5 ✉ Xichang'an Jie ☎ 6513 2255

🕐 Apr–Oct daily 8.30–5; Nov–Mar 8.30–4.30 🍴 Snack shop in the Imperial Garden 🚇 Tiananmen Xi, Tiananmen Dong 💰 Inexpensive (additional to entrance ticket to Forbidden City)

### SHENWU GATE

Shenwumen (Gate of Spiritual Prowess) is the northern gate of the Forbidden City, built in 1420. Each day, at dawn and dusk, the bell was rung 108 times, followed by the drum. Every three years, the girls selected as concubines used Shenwu to enter the palace. The tower, which gives good views across to Jingshan Park, can be reached by a long ramp. It contains an exhibition related to the architecture of the Forbidden City (explanations in Chinese only).

✚ G4 ✉ Jingshanqian Jie, Dongcheng District ☎ 6513 2255 🕐 Apr–Oct daily 8.30–5; Nov–Mar daily 8.30–4.30. Last admission tickets are sold 1 hour before closing 🍴 Snack shop in the Imperial Garden 🚇 Tiananmen Xi, Tiananmen Dong 🚫 None 💰 Moderate (included in entrance ticket to Forbidden City)

*Two grand halls within the Forbidden City*

# The Forbidden City

No longer forbidden territory, the vast imperial palace affords an insight into the lives of the emperors and their families and courts.

**DISTANCE:** 2.5 miles (4km)  **ALLOW:** 2 hours (not including stops)

**START**

**TIAN'ANMEN GATE**
 G6 Tiananmen Xi, Tiananmen Dong

**END**

**TIAN'ANMEN GATE**

**1** Cross over the moat by one of the marble bridges and go through the massive Tian'anmen Gate, passing the giant portrait of an ageless Chairman Mao.

**8** Beyond Wumen, approach the Tian'anmen Gate by way of a stroll through the gardens and pavilions of Zhongshan Park.

**2** To the right of the long approach way between the Duanmen and Wumen gates is the People's Cultural Park. Across another moat are the three great halls of the Taimiao (Imperial Ancestors Temple).

**7** The Gate of Earthly Tranquillity leads, appropriately, to the Imperial Garden (▷ 32–33) close to the north end of the palace complex. Keep to the right on the return, for a view from a different perspective.

**3** Now cross over the Palace Moat, continue through the Meridian Gate (Wumen, ▷ 36), and across the Golden Water River on one of the marble bridges, into the Forbidden City (▷ 24–25).

**6** Behind it are the halls of Middle Harmony (▷ 26–27) and Preserving Harmony (▷ 28–29). Descend to another courtyard and pass through the gate of Heavenly Purity, past a cluster of palaces and halls, including the Palace of Earthly Tranquillity.

**4** Directly ahead on the far side of a broad courtyard is the Gate of Supreme Harmony. Keeping to the right, you can admire the Tower of Manifest Benevolence.

**5** Climb the stairway up to the Hall of Supreme Harmony (▷ 30–31).

From the Forbidden City, south through Tian'anmen Square to the Temple of Heaven, stretches a part of Beijing that's rich in both historical and contemporary attractions, and in the local color of a fast-changing city.

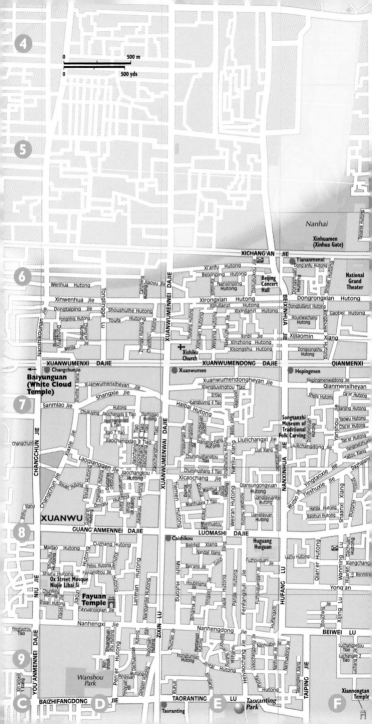

4

0    500 m
0    500 yds

5

*Nanhai*

**Xinhuamen (Xinhua Gate)**

XICHANG'AN JIE

6

Wenhua Hutong
Xinwenhua Jie
Dongtaiping Jie
Yongning Hutong
Shoushuihe Hutong
Toufa Hutong
Naoshikou'an
Tonglinge
Zhongjing Hutong

Xianfu Hutong
Beixinping Hutong
Jiaoyu Hutong
Nanxinping Hutong

XUANWUMENNEI DAJIE

Xirongxian Hutong
Xiliulianzi Hutong
Xixinlianzi Hutong

Youying Xiang
Xuan Hutong
Weiying Hutong

Xinbi Hutong
Xinzhong Hutong
Xisongshu Hutong

Tiananmenxi
Dong'anfu Hutong

**Beijing Concert Hall**

Dongrongxian Hutong
Dongliulianzi Hutong
Houxiwachang Hutong
Gaobei Hutong

BEIXINHUA JIE

✚ Xishiku Church

XUANWUMENDONG DAJIE

Xililaomin Xiang
Dongsonshu Hutong

**National Grand Theater**

QIANMENXI

XUANWUMENXI DAJIE
● Changchunjie

**Baiyunguan (White Cloud Temple)** ■

Naoshikounan
Dangjing Hutong
Wenhua

● Xuanwumen

Xuanwumendongheyan Jie

● Hepingmen

Hepingmenwaidong Jie

Xuanwumenxiheyan Jie
Shangxie Jie

Xianglvyingtou Tiao
Ertiao
Xianglvying 4 Tiao
Haibai Hutong

Qianmenxiheyan
Shelia Hutong
Da'er Hutong

**Songtanzhi Museum of Traditional Folk Carving**

7

CHANGCHUN JIE

Sanmiao Jie

Xiajie Jie
Chukuiying
Jiaochangda 6 Tiao
Jiaochangxiao
Xiao 7 Tiao
Jiaochangxiao 5 Tiao

Dazhaijia Hutong
Jingzhong Hutong

Liulichangxi Jie
Nanliu Xiang
Liuli Xiang
Nanliu Xiang

Liulichang Jie

Yaowu Hutong
Cha'er Hutong
Yan'er Hutong
Yangmeizhuxie
Qiaou Xiang

Changchun Hutong
Laojianggen Hutong
Xinan Hutong

Jiaochangkou
Hutong

NANXINHUA

Tieshuxie Jie
Yingtaoxie Jie
Wudao Tiao

Shaanxi Xiang
Dajiahang
Hanlia Hutong
Baishun Hutong

Changchun

Laojianggen Hutong
Dintai Hutong

XUANWUMENWAI DAJIE

Tiemen
Hutong

Chunshushangtou
Tiao
Chunshushang 3 Tiao
Xicaochang

Guangjuyuan Hutong
Qiansungongyuan Hutong
Lianglayuanbe
Lianglayuanbei Hutong
Qiansungongyuan
Hutong

8

XUANWU

Xishi

GUANG'ANMENNEI DAJIE
Cuzhang Hutong
Madao Hutong
Shuru Hutong
Chunpen
Hutong

● Caishikou

**Ox Street Mosque** 
Niujie Libai Si
**Fayuan Temple** ■
Fayuanslqian Jie

Peiyu Hutong
Fayuanshou Jie

Lamman
Nanbinma Hutong

Beidall Xiang
Nandall Xiang
Bao'ansi Jie
Houbinma Hutong

LUOMASHI DAJIE

**Huguang Huiguan**

Lazhu Hutong
Qian er Hutong

Xiangchang
Xianchang

Renmin

Yong an

HUFANG LU

BEIWEI LU

9

NIU JIE

Xianglie 1 Xiang

Nanhengxi Jie
Shuangzha Hutong
Chuchanbe Hutong
Pen'er Hutong
Pingyuanli

YOU'ANMENNEI DAJIE

Nanhengdong Jie
Hongtumian Hutong

Nanhuabei Jie

Nanhengdong Jie
Heiyaochang Jie

**Wanshou Park**

Weishoul
Hutong

Nanheng
Hutong

TAORANTING LU

TAIPING JIE

**Xian%Q**

Yingtaotou
Tiao

● Yingtaodou
Xiang

BAIZHIFANGDONG JIE

ZIXIN LU

**Taoranting Park**
● Taoranting

Luchangjietou
Tiao
Luchangjie 2
Tiao

**XianNS ntan Temple**

C        D        E        F

Dengshikouxi Jie
Dengshikou Dajie
Dengshikou
Donghuangchengen Jie
Baishu Hutong
Shaoliu Hutong
Xitangzi Hutong
Xila Hutong
Ganyu Hutong
Donghuamen Dajie
Dong'anmen Dajie
Jinyu Hutong
Meizha Hutong

Pudu Temple
Caichang Hutong
Chenguang
Beishuaifu Hutong
Daruanfu Hutong
Datianshuijing Hutong
Shuaifuyuan Hutong
Beiwanzi
Duanku Hutong
Dongdan 3 Tiao
Nanguanchang Hutong
Xiagongfu Jie
Dongdan 2 Tiao

Zhongshan Park
Park of the People's Culture
Changpuheyan
Tian'anmen Gate (Gate of Heavenly Peace)
Former Imperial Archive
Sun Yat-sen Park

DONGCHANG'AN JIE
Tiananmendong
Wangfujing
Dongdan
Dongdan Park

Tian'anmen Square
TAIJICHANG DAJIE
Taijichangtou Tiao
Taijichang 2 Tiao

Renmin Dahui Tang (Great Hall of the People)
National Museum of China
Taijichang 3 Tiao
Dahua
42

Monument to the People's Heroes
Xindalu
Dongjiaomin Xiang
Beijing Police Museum
Dongjiaomin Xiang

Mao Zhuxi Jinian Tang (Chairman Mao Memorial Hall)
Zhengyangmen (Qianmen Gate)

DAJIE
QIANMENDONG DAJIE
CHONGWENMENXI DAJIE

Qianmen
Jianlou
Beijing Planning Exhibition Hall
Qianmennanhe'an
Chongwenmenxiheyan
Qianmennanhe'an

Qian Xiang Yi Silk Store
Chongwenmenxihe'an
Dongdamochang
Xidamochang
Xlyue Hutong
Jinmao Hutong
Dougu Hutong
Dongxinglong Jie

Qianmenxiheyan Jie
Paizi Hutong
Gongji Hutong
Langfangtou Tiao
Langfang 2 Tiao
Xianyukou
Xixinglong Jie
Dashilan
Dajilla Hutong
Wangpi Hutong
Shilla Hutong
Liangshidian
Buxiangzi Hutong
Caochangheng Hutong
Yunju Hutong

Peiying Hutong
ZHUSHIKOUDONG DAJIE
Dongbanbi Jie
Jinxiutong Jie
CHONGWEN
Dongxiaoshi

Xiaoweihing Hutong
Tao'er Hutong
Dashi Hutong
Santiao
Shilidaozi Hutong
Xixiaoshi Jie
Qinghua Jie

Tianchang Hutong
Liuxue Lu
Chuziying Hutong
Xlyuanxi
Xlyuanxi
Longrugou Lu

TIANTAN LU
TIANTAN LU

Fuchangnei Jie
Ertiao
Fuchangle 3 Tiao
Zhongshull
Double Ring Longevity Pavilion

TIANQIAONAN DAJIE
Beijing Museum of Natural History
Chinese Rose Garden
Qi'niandian (Qinian Hall)

Wutiao
Liutiao
Nanwei Lu
Zhaigong (Hall of Abstinence)
Tiantan (Temple of Heaven)
Huangqiong Yu (Imperial Vault of Heaven)

YONGDINGMENNEI DAJIE
Fukangli

G
H
J

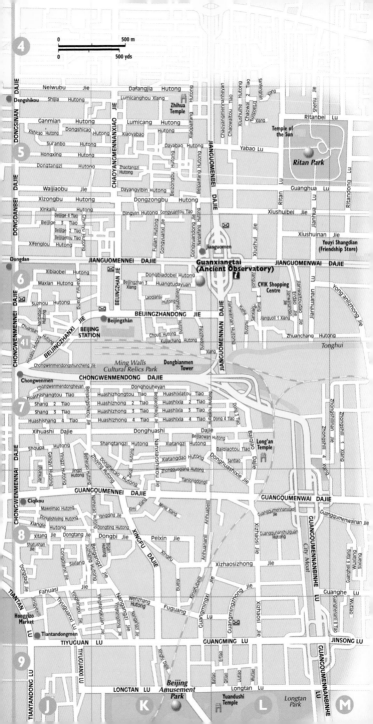

**4**

0    500 m

0    500 yds

Neiwubu        Jie

Dafangjia    Hutong

Lumicanghou Xiang

**DONGSI NAN DAJIE**

Dengshikou  Shijia   Hutong

Ganmian         Hutong

Xizhao Hutong   Dongshicao   Hutong

Suierbing    Hutong

Hongxing    Hutong

**5**

Dongtangzi    Hutong

Waijiaobu       Jie

**DONGDAN BEI DAJIE**

Xizongbu     Hutong

Xinkailu      Hutong

Beijie 4 Tiao

Beijie  3  Tiao

Beijie  2  Tiao

Beijiaotou Tiao

Xifenglou   Hutong

Lumicang      Hutong

Xiaoyabao

Dayabao   Hutong

Zhaotangzi
Hutong

Dayangyibin Hutong

Dongzongbu   Hutong

Dingyin Hutong   Dongyuantou Tiao

Fujian  Hutong

**CHAOYANGMENNANXIAO JIE**

**JIANGUOMENBEI DAJIE**

Zhihua
Temple

Chaoyangmennanheyan

Chaowaitou Tiao

Chaowai   Tiao

Xiushuihe   Hutong

Xiang

Neiwantou   Xiang

Yabao   Lu

Ritanbei    Lu

**Temple
of the Sun**

**Ritan Park**

Guanghua    Lu

Ritan

Xiushuibei    Jie

Xiushuinan    Jie

**Youyi Shangdian
(Friendship Store)**

Ritan

Ritandong   Lu

**Dongdan**

**JIANGUOMENNEI       DAJIE**

Jianguomen

**JIANGUOMENWAI  DAJIE**

**6**

Xibiaobei   Hutong

Maxian    Hutong

**DONGDAN BEI DAJIE**

Suzhou    Hutong

Nanjuchao
Hutong

Chuanbei

**BEIJINGZHAN XI JIE**

**BEIJINGZHAN JIE**

Beijingzhan 3
Xiang

Dongbiaobei  Hutong

Huangtudayuan

Laoqianju

**Guanxiangtai
(Ancient Observatory)**

Beijing 3 Tiao

Chunsong
Hutong

**JIANGUOMENNAN DAJIE**

Jianguomenwai

Dongerhuan

Yong'anlizhong   Lu

**CVIK Shopping
Centre**

Yong'andongli

Jianguoli 2 Xiang

Jianguoli 1 Xiang

Zhuanchang    Hutong

**BEIJINGZHANDONG    JIE**

**41**

**CHONGWENMENNEI DAJIE**

Beijingzhan

**BEIJING
STATION**

Choudi   Hutong

Kuijiachang   Hutong

**Ming Walls
Cultural Relics Park**

Chongwenmendonghuncheng Jie

Paofangnan

**Dongbianmen
Tower**

Tonghui

Zhuanchang   Hutong

**Chongwenmen**

**CHONGWENMENDONG    DAJIE**

Chongwenmendongheyan

Donghouheyan

**7**

Huashishangtou Tiao

Shang    1   Tiao

Shang    3   Tiao

Huashishang  4  Tiao

Beiyangshicun  Hutong

Huashizhong   Tiao

Huashizhong  2  Tiao

Huashizhong  3  Tiao

Huashizhong  4  Tiao

Huashixiatou Tiao

Huashixia   Tiao

Huashixia  2  Tiao

Huashixia  3  Tiao

Huashixia  4  Tiao

Dong 4 Tiao

**CHONGWENMENNEI DAJIE**

Xihuashi   Dajie

Shoupa    Hutong

Ganyu Hutong

Yingzi Hutong

Jingzi
Hutong

Zhufang Hutong

Dongchadao  Hutong

Zhuling Hutong

Shangtangzi Hutong

Xiatangzi Hutong

**Donghuashi      Dajie**

Nanxiashao Jie

Xiatangdao   Hutong

Zhongxuogliang Hutong

Tianlongdong

Beijiaowan Hutong

Baidiaotou  Hutong

Santiao

**Long'an
Temple**

Baidao
Dajie

Zhongshinan  Jie

Zhongshi  1  Xiang

**GUANGOUMENNEI        DAJIE**

Ciqikou

Mawelmao Hutong

Dongjishiving Hutong

**Xiangle**

Xitang   Jie

Shatushan
Jie

**8**

**CHONGWENMENNEI DAJIE**

Dongtang Jie

Congdianxi Jie

Xihuan Hutong

Sixiang

Bi'an
Hutong

Beigangzi
Jie

**Dongbi**

**XINGFU DAJIE**

Peixin    Jie

Xingfu

Xingfu

Ximi

Ming   Xiang

Anhuanli

Anhuanlil

Xizhaosizhong   Jie

Xizhaosizhong

Guangqumenxi   Jie

Guangqumennanxi  Jie

Guangqumenxishuiguan
Hutong

**GUANGOUMENWAI  DAJIE**

**City Moat**

Guanghe   Lu

Guanghe  2  Xiang  & 1  Tiao

Wuruo

**GUANGOUMENNANBINHE**

**TIANTAN**

Fahuasi

Dongdenglixi Jie

Dongxinglong  Hutong

Yingtaodong Jie

Tiyuguanxi Jie

**Hongqiao
Market**

Tiantandongmen

**TIANTANDONG LU**

**TIYUGUAN LU**

**TIYUGUANXI LU**

Sixiang Jie

Nanglangxia Jie

Nangyangli Jie

Wenzhang
Hutong

Fuguang

Guangmingyinli

Guangmingzhong   Jie

Xizhaosi   Jie

Xizhaosi

**GUANGMING LU**

Longtan

Yingti   Dajie

Yingti
Dajie

Yandu

Miao

Longtan    Hutong

Wudao

Sanjingtiao   Jie

**GUANGOUMENNANBINHE LU**

**JINSONG LU**

**9**

**LONGTAN LU**

**Beijing
Amusement
Park**

**Yuandushi
Temple**

**LONGTAN LU**

**Longtan
Park**

**J**        **K**        **L**        **M**

# Ancient Observatory

*View of modern Beijing from the rooftop of the Observatory (left); armillary sphere (right)*

**Explore centuries of astronomy in China through the range of star-gazing paraphernalia on display here in a corner tower of the city's walls. There are fine city views from the roof.**

**Viewing the skies** In the 13th century Kublai Khan founded an observatory near the present site, building on a Chinese tradition that was already well established. Islamic scientists were in charge in the early 17th century and when Jesuit missionaries arrived in Beijing they astonished the court by their ability to make astronomical forecasts and soon found themselves in charge of the observatory. New instruments were installed, and the Jesuits remained until the early 19th century. In 1900, French and German troops stole many of the instruments; they were later returned.

**What to see** At street level, on the other side of the entrance booth, a small open-air area displays reproductions of various astronomical instruments. Also on street level is a small museum with explanations (in English) of the main exhibits. These include a copy of the world's oldest surviving formal astronomical account, a 14th-century record of a supernova. Steps lead up to the top of the tower, and on the roof there are eight original instruments—including a sextant, a theodolite, a quadrant and an altazimuth—most made in the 17th century. Back at street level, the small rear garden contains more reproductions of celestial instruments as well as stone carvings recording constellations and solar eclipses.

## THE BASICS

+ K6
⊠ 2 Dongbiaobei Hutong, Jianguomennei Dajie
☎ 6524 2202
🕐 Apr–Sep daily 9–5; Oct–Mar 9–11, 1–4
Ⓜ Jianguomen
🚌 1, 4, 9, 10, 43, 103, 403
♿ None
💷 Inexpensive

## HIGHLIGHTS

● 4,500-year-old pottery jar with pictographic solar patterns
● Star map from Song dynasty (13th century)
● Equatorial armillary sphere of 1673
● Views of the city from the roof of the tower

# Chairman Mao Memorial Hall

The Memorial Hall illuminated at night (left); crowds of visitors outside the building (right)

## THE BASICS

🗺 G6
✉ South end of Tian'anmen Square
☎ 6513 2277
🕐 Sep–Jun Tue–Sun 8.30–11.30, 2–4; Jul, Aug Tue–Sun 8.30–11.30
🚇 Qianmen
🚌 1, 4, 10, 22, 203
🎫 Free, but must show passport

## HIGHLIGHTS

● The embalmed corpse of China's first Communist leader
● Watching the respectful crowds shuffling in and out

## DID YOU KNOW?

● The government overruled Mao's wish to be cremated.
● 5 gallons (22 liters) of formaldehyde went into Mao's corpse.

**Millions of ordinary Chinese still have a deep respect for Mao Zedong. A visit to his mausoleum makes this very obvious. Chinese citizens wait for hours to file silently past Mao's preserved remains.**

**Exterior** The Memorial Hall, behind the Monument to the People's Heroes at the south end of Tian'anmen Square, was completed in 1977 by volunteer labor, only one year after the death of the famous helmsman of the Chinese people. To date, it has seen more than 120 million visitors. The calligraphy of the inscription above the entrance, "Chairman Mao Mausoleum," was the work of Hua Guofeng who briefly succeeded Mao to the leadership of the Communist Party. The two-tiered structure is supported by 44 octagonal granite columns.

**Interior** Entry to the hallowed ground is through a vast anteroom dominated by a large statue of Mao. The line of visitors moves forward inexorably into the main memorial hall, where the embalmed body lies in a crystal coffin in a gloomy orange light, draped with the red flag of the Chinese Communist Party. You are permitted a couple of minutes to file past the coffin. Photography is strictly forbidden (it costs 10 yuan to check in your camera). The body is raised from its freezer each morning and descends after the last of the morning pilgrims. Stories regarding the problems of maintaining the body gained credence in 1998, when the mausoleum reopened after a nine-month "renovation"—looking the same as ever.

# National Museum of China

*Counting down the seconds to the Beijing Olympics (right) at the National Museum of China (middle, left)*

北京2008年奥运会
Beijing 2008 Olympic Games

距 2008 年 8 月 8 日开幕
From the opening ceremony on August 8th,2008

倒计时 | 天
Countdown | days

**In 2005 work began on a major revamp of the building dominating the eastern side of Tian'anmen Square, merging the Museum of the Chinese Revolution and the Chinese History Museum, which currently occupy it. Work is expected to be complete by the end of 2012.**

**Blowing away the cobwebs** The Chinese government is investing an estimated 1.8 billion yuan (US$217.65 million) in the expansion and refurbishment of this new cultural landmark. The shell of the existing building will remain more or less intact, but the imposing 327-yard (300m) facade will extend for an additional 76 yards (70m) along the eastern side of Tian'anmen Square. This will double the existing floor space of 101,659sq yards (85,000sq m). The facilities will include a reception area for visitors, a digital cinema, car parking and shops, as well as a research facility and around two-dozen exhibition halls covering Chinese history (including Revolutionary history), art and folk art. During the reconstruction the museum hopes to be able to offer visitors a taster in the form of temporary exhibitions, but there is likely to be considerable disruption.

**What to expect** The former Museum of Chinese History was founded in 1918, but most of its holdings were acquired after the Communist Revolution. Of the 600,000 artifacts in the museum, visitors can expect to see Neolithic tools, Han dynasty pottery, Ming vases, jade and lacquerware, silk embroidery and ornamental jewelry.

## THE BASICS

www.nationalmuseum.cn

➕ G6

✉ 16 Dongchang'an Jie, east side of Tian'anmen Square

☎ 6513 2801

🕐 Jul–Aug, 1st week of May and Oct daily 8–6; Sep–Jun daily 8.30–4.30

🚇 Tiananmen Dong

🚌 1, 4, 17, 57

## HIGHLIGHTS

● The monumental facade facing Tian'anmen Square
● Electronic sign outside which counts down the days, hours, minutes and seconds to the Olympic opening ceremony on August 8, 2008

# Qianmen Gate

## HIGHLIGHTS

The view from the top of the gate takes in:
● Chairman Mao Memorial Hall (immediately to the south, ▷ 44)
● Tian'anmen Square (to the south, ▷ 52)
● Great Hall of the People (west, ▷ 55)
● National Museum of China (east, ▷ 45)

## TIP

● Outdoors are stone tables for picnics.

**Emperors took their security very seriously—a moat and a large wall ringed the outside of their private city. The remaining portal of Qianmen Gate (Zhengyangmen) gives a sense of Tian'anmen Square's monumental scale.**

No entry Access to the Forbidden City was simply not an option for the general public under imperial rule; access to the inner city was controlled by a series of nine guarded gates. On the south side of Beijing, Zhengyangmen was the main point of transit between the inner city and the residential areas outside.

City gates The gate was constructed during the rule of Emperor Yongle (ruled 1403–24) in the first half of the 15th century. A sister gate (Jianlou)

*Detail of the intricately carved roof of the imposing Qianmen Gate (left); the Arrow Tower (right)*

is clearly visible across the street to the south but, unlike Zhengyangmen, it is not open to the public. Originally, these two gates were joined by walls.

**Visiting Qianmen Gate** When you stand with the Chairman Mao Memorial Hall behind you, the ticket booth is on the corner of the left side of the gate, right next to the entrance. Inside, there are three levels. On the first is a gallery of black-and-white photographs relating to Chinese history, with brief explanations in English. The second is filled with fairly uninspiring souvenir stores, and on the third level there is a more interesting store with items devoted to tea-drinking. Facing the Qianmen Gate to the south is a second gate, the Jianlou, or Arrow Gate, which like its companion across the way dates from the Ming dynasty. However, the Jianlou cannot be visited.

**THE BASICS**

✚ G7
✉ Tian'anmen Square
🕐 Daily 8.30–4
🍴 Western take-out fast food is available across the street opposite Qianmen subway station
🚇 Qianmen
🚍 1, 17
♿ None
💷 Inexpensive

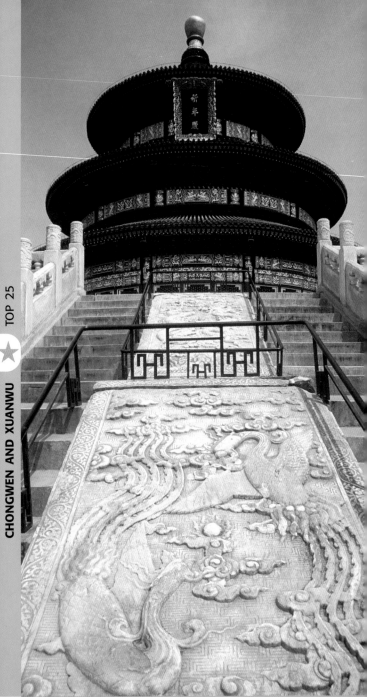

*External views of the beautiful Qinian Hall, built in the early 15th century*

# Qinian Hall

**Through the perfection and harmony of its proportions, this triple-roofed temple achieves a state of both ultramodernism and sacred serenity. It represents the highest development of religious architecture in China.**

**Heavenly sacrifices** Qinian Hall, or Hall of Prayer for Good Harvests, is part of Tiantan, the Temple of Heaven (▷ 50–51), the largest group of temple buildings in China. Tiantan Park surrounds the temple off the north–south axis that aligns the major buildings in the Forbidden City.

Ming and Qing emperors ceremoniously traveled the short journey south to Tiantan to offer sacrifices to heaven in springtime and at the winter solstice. Before the first Ming emperor made this sacred journey in the 15th century, this area was associated with religious rituals as far back as the Zhou dynasty (11th century BC–256BC).

**Floating skyward** First built in 1420 and completely restored in 1889 after a lightning strike, the hall is an extraordinary structure—three stories and a three-tiered roof, with blue-glazed tiles, rising above marble terraces and seeming to float in the air. The four central columns, the Dragon Fountain pillars, represent the four seasons, and the outer rings, of 12 columns each, represent the months of the year and the 12 divisions of the day or "watches." The complex artwork of the caisson ceiling, with a wood-sculptured dragon in the center, is best appreciated with binoculars.

## THE BASICS

➕ H9
✉ Tiantandong Lu, Chongwen District
☎ 6702 8866
🕐 May–Oct daily 6am–9pm; Nov–Apr daily 6am–8pm
🚌 6, 15, 17, 20, 35, 39, 43, 106
♿ Cobbled ramp at the west entrance to street level
💰 Moderate; park inexpensive
❓ Audio tours

## HIGHLIGHTS

● Dragon Fountain pillars
● Intricate ceiling sculptures
● Large arts and crafts store in the courtyard, south of the hall

# Temple of Heaven

**HIGHLIGHTS**

**HIGHLIGHTS**

● Bridge of Vermilion Stairs leading to the Imperial Vault of Heaven
● Coffered ceiling of the Imperial Vault of Heaven
● Echo Wall and Echo Stones
● View of the Imperial Vault from the top tier of the Circular Mound Altar

**Here, Ming emperors clothed in sacrificial robes consulted their ancestors' tablets before ceremonially ascending the steps of the three-tiered Circular Mound Altar and reading sacred prayers and performing rituals that had been refined over the centuries.**

**Wooden temple** From the Gate of Prayer for Good Harvests, a raised walkway leads to the Imperial Vault of Heaven. Constructed entirely of wood, it is an octagonal vault with a double-eaved roof. Dating originally from 1530, it was rebuilt in the mid-17th century. In many respects it is a smaller version of the Qinian Hall, with a similar blue-tiled roof to represent heaven, but it receives more light so it's easier to appreciate the elegant art inside.

Visitors outside the Imperial Vault of Heaven (left); a man listening at the Echo Wall (bottom left); view of the Imperial Vault of Heaven from the Circular Mound Altar (bottom right); visitors examining the Circular Mound Altar (right)

**Echoes and more echoes** Surrounding the Imperial Vault of Heaven is the Echo Wall, whose acoustic properties allow two people standing next to it to converse at a distance. In the courtyard at the foot of the staircase, the first stone is said to generate one echo, the second stone two echoes, and the third three echoes.

**Circular Mound Altar (Huanquitan)** This huge round altar is not as impressive as the other buildings of Tiantan, but its symbolism is highly charged and it is the Altar of Heaven itself. The three marble tiers symbolize earth, man and heaven and, according to Chinese cosmology, the central stone in the top tier marks the center of the world. On the winter solstice, the emperor ascended to this spot and from a stone tablet read sacred prayers of indulgence.

## THE BASICS

- ✚ H9
- ✉ Tiantandong Lu, Chongwen District
- ☎ 6702 8866
- 🕐 May–Oct daily 6am–9pm; Nov–Apr daily 6am–8pm
- 🚌 6, 15, 17, 20, 35, 39, 43, 106
- ♿ None
- 🎫 Entrance charge included in ticket for Qinian Hall
- ❓ Audio tours

# Tian'anmen Square

TOP 25

## HIGHLIGHTS

● Chairman Mao Memorial Hall (south, ▷ 44)
● Great Hall of the People (west, ▷ 55)
● National Museum of China (east, ▷ 45)
● Monument to the People's Heroes (center, ▷ 55)

## TIP

● A significant number of seemingly innocuous Chinese tourists in the square are actually plainclothes policemen, there to pounce instantly on any kind of demonstration, indigenous or foreign, and arrest the demonstrators.

**Kite-flyers and street vendors throng the world's largest square, giving it a festive air, while the monumental architecture is a reminder that the most momentous events in modern Chinese history have taken place here.**

**A 20th-century gesture** People had gathered outside Tian'anmen Gate since the mid-17th century—it was here that Beijingers assembled in 1949 to hear the declaration of the People's Republic. Today's vast square, some 2,400ft (800m) long by 1,650ft (500m) wide, was not formally laid out until the 1950s. Vast rallies launched the Cultural Revolution from here in the 1960s, and in 1976 the deaths of Mao and Zhou Enlai (Chinese premier from 1949 until his death) brought millions of mourners to this spot. Then,

Revolutionary statue flanking Chairman Mao Memorial Hall (left); a portrait of Mao above the entrance to the Forbidden City (middle); a portrait of the revolutionary Sun Yat Sen (right); crowds approaching the square (bottom left); children flying a kite (bottom middle); Tian'anmen Gate with fountains in the foreground (bottom right)

for two months beginning in April 1989, the square became the focus for the most serious threat to Communist rule since its creation. In June 1989, the government sent in troops and tanks to bring student protests to a violent end. Thousands are believed to have died. The square is now the site for occasional suppressed protests.

**Tian'anmen Gate** When China was under imperial rule, Tian'anmen Gate formed the first entrance to the Forbidden City and served as the ritually ordained point for the emperor's edicts to be made public. As such, it seemed an appropriate platform for Chairman Mao Zedong's announcement, on October 1, 1949, to the waiting crowd and to the world at large, that "the Chinese people have now stood up." A giant portrait of Chairman Mao hangs above the central portal.

## THE BASICS

🞦 G6
🚇 Tiananmen Xi, Tiananmen Dong
🚌 1, 4, 10, 22, 203
♿ None
🖐 Free

**Tian'anmen Gate**
🞦 G6
🕐 Daily 8–5
🖐 Moderate (free to pass through)

# More to See

## BEIJING AMUSEMENT PARK

Here, in the southwest of the city, on the west side of Longtan Lake Park, is an impressive range of fun rides— Ferris wheel, roller coaster, waterslide, boat rides and shooting arcades.

✚ K9  ⊠ 1 Zuoanmen Nei Dajie, Longtan Lake Park, Chongwen District  ☎ 6711 1155  ⏱ Daily 9–5  🚇 Chongwenmen, then bus 8  ♿ None  💷 Expensive

## BEIJING MUSEUM OF NATURAL HISTORY

This place is unique and very strange. The ground floor, devoted to zoology, is by turns dull and kitschy, but up-stairs, under the guise of anthropological study, there are displays of cross sections of human cadavers and pickled organs.

✚ G9  ⊠ 126 Tianqiaonan Lu, Chongwen District  ☎ 6702 4431  ⏱ Tue–Sun 8.30–5 (last ticket 4)  🚌 2, 25, 53, 59, 120, 803, or Qianmen subway and bus 209  ♿ None  💷 Inexpensive

## FAYUAN TEMPLE

This delightful Buddhist temple, with its six lilac-decked courtyards, is now a college for novice monks. The first temple on this site was founded in AD645, and earlier buildings served many purposes, including that of an examination hall. Look for the display of illustrated moralizing texts on the right side as you go through the hall leading to the main temple building.

✚ D9  ⊠ 7 Fayuansi/Quianjie, Xuanwu District  ☎ 6353 3966  ⏱ Thu–Tue 8.30–11.30, 1.30–3.30  🚌 61, 109  🚇 Xuanwumen  ♿ None  💷 Inexpensive

## GRAND VIEW GARDENS (DAGUANYUAN PARK)

Laid out in the 1980s as part of a project to film the 18th-century classic Chinese novel *The Dream of the Red Mansion*, this is a pleasant place away from the city center, with a strange artificial rock formation, a water pavilion and walkways around a lake.

✚ Off map, south of C9  ⊠ Nancaiyuan Jie, Xuanwu District  ☎ 6354 4994  ⏱ Daily 8.30–4.30  🚌 12, 19, 59  ♿ None  💷 Inexpensive

*Enjoying the rides at Beijing Amusement Park*

*Dinosaur skeletons at Beijing Museum of Natural History*

## GREAT HALL OF THE PEOPLE

The vast Great Hall of the People effectively takes up the west side of Tian'anmen Square. Barring a session of the People's Congress—an infrequent event—the hall is open to the public. It was built in the late 1950s, and the monolithic architecture betrays its Stalinist origins. The rooms are cavernous and forbiddingly gray in color and mood. There are some 30 reception rooms, each named after a region or city and decorated in a style appropriate to that area; some are open to public view.

➕ F6 ✉ West side of Tian'anmen Square
☎ 6309 6156 🕐 Daily 8.30–3.30
🚇 Tiananmen Xi 🚌 1, 17 ♿ None
🚻 Moderate

## MONUMENT TO THE PEOPLE'S HEROES

This monument, the central point in Tian'anmen Square, is dedicated to all those who struggled for the glorious revolution. The site carries a warning to the effect that anyone trying to start another one will be sternly punished. The foundations of the 125ft-high (38m) granite and marble obelisk were laid on the eve of October 1, 1949—the day that the establishment of the People's Republic was announced—but the monument was not officially unveiled to the public until 1958. The base of the monument is decorated with a series of bas-reliefs depicting key scenes from China's revolutionary history. The platform upon which the obelisk stands is now closed off to the public and kept under guard—a sign indicates that any laying of wreaths or commemorative gestures is strictly outlawed, as this has led to uprisings in the past, notably in 1976 at the death of the immensely popular Zhou Enlai.

➕ G6 ✉ Tian'anmen Square
🚇 Tiananmen Xi 🚌 1, 4, 10, 22, 203
♿ None 🚻 Free

## RITAN PARK

Ritan (Temple of the Sun) Park developed out of a 16th-century altar site where the emperor made sacrificial offerings to the sun god. In the heart of

Great Hall of the People

Monument to the People's Heroes

embassy-land, near the Friendship Store (▷ 58) and the Russian market, it makes for a pleasant evening stroll.

➕ L5 ✉ Ritan Lu, Chaoyang District ☎ 8563 5438 🕐 6.30am–8.30pm 🚌 1, 4, 9, 29, 48, 57, 103 ♿ Few 💲 Inexpensive

## TAORANTING PARK

The first park here was laid out in the Liao period (947–1125) and during the Qing dynasty it became one of the few parks open to the public. Its swimming pool is a big draw for Chinese families, but there are quiet places to retreat to, including the remains of a monastery and a number of pavilions (this is also known as Joyous Pavilion Park).

➕ E9 and off map to south ✉ 19 Taiping Jie, Xuanwu District ☎ 6353 2385 🕐 6am–10pm 🚌 14 from Hepingmen subway or 59 from Qianmen ♿ None 💲 Inexpensive

## TUANJIEHU PARK

This delightful little park, surrounded by high-rise office blocks and off the tourist trail, offers a relaxing diversion

from palaces and stores. Paths lead through a scenic arrangement of lake, willow trees, humped bridge and greenery. There is a small amusement park with rides for toddlers.

➕ Off map, east of M4 ✉ 16 Tuanjiehu Nanlu, Chaoyang District ☎ 8597 3603 🕐 6.30am–9pm 🚌 43, 115 ♿ Few 💲 Inexpensive

## WHITE CLOUD TEMPLE

The oldest Taoist temple in Beijing, the White Cloud Temple (Baiyunguan) was founded in the Tang dynasty (8th century). The largest of the prayer halls commemorates Founder Qiu, who was invited to run the monastery by Genghis Khan in the 13th century. Perhaps the finest artwork in the temple is *Founder Qiu's Visit to the West*, a wonderfully vivid depiction of his caravan of followers traveling across the mountains. Look out too for stone carvings of Taoist symbols, including chickens, cranes and mushrooms.

➕ B6 ✉ 6 Baiyunguan Jie, Xuanwu District ☎ 6346 3531 🕐 Daily 8.30–4 🚇 Nanlishilu ♿ Few 💲 Inexpensive

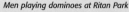
*A wall painting in White Cloud Temple*

*Men playing dominoes at Ritan Park*

# Xuanwu Temples

This walk takes in a more remote part of Xuanwu, which is being redeveloped but still has old streets and sights of historical interest.

**DISTANCE:** 2.8 miles (4.5km)     **ALLOW:** 3 hours, including sights

START

**CHANGCHUN JIE**
🚇 D7 🚉 Changchunjie

END

**CHANGCHUN JIE**

**1** From the metro station, walk south on the west side of busy Changchun Jie. At the first big intersection, go right (west) into quieter Huaibaishu Jie, and walk a few hundred yards (meters) to the entrance to Xuanwu Art Garden.

**2** Stroll through the tranquil park. With its well-tended gardens, dense tree cover, small central lake, pavilions and sheltered corridors, it forms an oasis of calm.

**3** Residents of the busy surrounding neighborhood exercise, read and play board games here. Exit on the park's south side.

**4** Go south through the old *hutong* district on Baoguosi Dongjiadao to the entrance to the Confucian Baoguo Temple, founded during the Liao dynasty (10th–12th century).

**8** Explore what remains of the *hutong* district surrounding the temple. Return to the intersection with Niu Jie, and take bus 38 or 61 back to Changchunjie metro station.

**7** This area is the heart of Bejing's Muslim community. Cross over to the east side of the street, to the 10th-century Niujie Mosque, which has the style of a Chinese temple. Continue south on Niu Jie to its intersection with Nanhengxi Jie. Go left, along to the gardens at the entrance to Fayuan Temple (▷ 54).

**6** Outside the temple, drop down to Guang'anmennei Dajie, the next main street to the south, and go left (east) along it to its intersection with Changchun Jie, where you go right into Niu Jie (Ox Street).

**5** Visit the colorful flea market which is held daily in the temple grounds.

# Shopping

## ARTS & CRAFTS STORE

This store in the prestigious China World Trade Center retails fine china, carpets and an array of expensive *objets d'art*.
➕ Off map, east of M6 ✉ 1 Jianguomenwai Dajie, Chaoyang District ☎ 6505 2261 🕐 Daily 9.20am–9.40pm 🚇 Guomao 🚌 1, 4, 37, 52

## BEIJING JADE CARVING FACTORY

The wide selection of jadeware here includes examples of this renowned Chinese handicraft in a luggage-friendly size. Look carefully at some of the finer items, noticing how cleverly the differing shades of green are used.
➕ L9 ✉ 11 Guangming Lu, Chongwen District ☎ 6702 7371 🕐 Daily 9–5 🚇 Jianguomen

## CHINA WORLD SHOPPING MALL

Among the chic boutiques and lifestyle stores is a well-stocked arts and crafts store, a useful deli, a drugstore and a large branch of the Hong Kong supermarket chain, Wellcome, which stocks an excellent range of local and Western foods.
➕ Off map, east of M6 ✉ 1 Jianguomenwai Dajie, Chaoyang District ☎ 6505 2288 🕐 Daily 9.30–9.30 🚇 Guomao 🚌 1, 4, 37, 52

## FRIENDSHIP STORE

There are four levels in this store; all but the second floor offer a good range of arts and crafts: jade, porcelain, cloisonné, lacquerware, silk, linen, paintings, carpets, works of calligraphy and kites. You'll find clothing on the second floor. There is a terrific choice of silk by the yard, and the selection of traditional Chinese dress is worth a look. Come here and check the prices before trying your hand at bargaining in street markets.
➕ M6 ✉ 17 Jianguomenwai Dajie, Chaoyang District ☎ 6500 3311 🕐 Daily 9.30–8.30 🚌 1, 2, 3, 4, 9, 802

## HONGQIAO MARKET

In the central area on the third floor, freshwater pearls are made into jewelry on the spot to customers' wishes. There are no fixed prices, so bargaining is required. Experts rub two pearls together; the rougher the contact the better; if they rub together smoothly the pearls are of poorer quality. Arts and crafts stores share the same floor: Nos. 213–14 and 218 specialize in cloisonné; No. 219 is devoted to finely crafted gilded-silver ornaments. Seek out the antiques shops also on the third floor. Much of the merchandise is reproduction. Shop No. 6 specializes in old clocks. Bear in mind when bargaining that these stores sell primarily to tourists.
➕ J9 ✉ 16 Hongqiao Lu, Chongwen District ☎ 6713 3354 🕐 Daily 9–6 🚌 36, 39, 43

## HUAXIA ARTS & CRAFTS BRANCH STORE

The second floor of this government store retails clocks, pocket watches, rugs, chinaware and woodcarvings from temples. Most of them are probably fake, but at least they look authentic.
➕ H5 ✉ 122 Liulichangdong Jie, Xuanwu District ☎ 6513 6204 🕐 Daily 9–7 🚇 Qianmen

## KERRY CENTRE

Though smaller and less exclusive than China World Shopping Mall (▷ left), this mall contains an excellent range of shops, from boutiques and hairdressers to

---

### SPOTTING FAKES

Check the bottoms and insides of antiques for clues about the antiquity—recent imitations are rarely finished on the underside of a drawer, for example, so you'll be able to spot the new plywood. Inspect seams and search for extra buttons (a luxury that real designers provide, but knockoff manufacturers neglect). If you can tell the real McCoy from a fake, the sales clerk can tell you're the real McCoy too—and will be more likely to quote you the right price.

aromatherapy stores and wine retailers.

🚇 Off map, east of M5 ✉ 1 Guanghua Lu, Chaoyang District ☎ 8529 8228 🕐 Daily 9–9 🚇 Guomao 🚌 48, 908

### LIULICHANG JIE

Conveniently located southwest of Qianmen, this famous old street— now renovated to look its age—is well worth a visit even if you buy nothing. Fine antiques stores stock woodblock print reproductions, porcelain, jade, snuff bottles, paintings and a few genuine antique pieces. Bargaining in this area is limited.

🚇 E/F7 ✉ Liulichangdong Jie, Xuanwu District 🕐 Daily 9–6 🚇 Qianmen

### PANJIAYUAN MARKET

Come here early on weekends, especially Sundays; by afternoon this market is already winding down. Most of the "antiques" are fake, but they are quality fakes and gratifying purchases may be made if you bargain rigorously. Never pay anything like the first price quoted. It is best to arrive by taxi, but make sure the taxi driver doesn't just drop you by the stands selling worthless bric-a-brac—ask your hotel to specify that you want to go to the antiques part of the market.

🚇 Off map, southeast of M9 ✉ Huawei Lu Dajie,

Dongsanhuan, Chaoyang District 🕐 Daily 8–1 🚌 35, 41

### QIANMEN CARPET COMPANY

This is one of the largest antique carpet dealers in Beijing. There are some very expensive antique carpets from Xinjiang and Tibet, as well as hand-made imitations and Henan silk carpets—the objectives of most visitors. The showroom is a converted air-raid shelter dating from the 1960s.

🚇 K9 ✉ 1st Floor, Building 3, Tiantan Mansion, 59 Xingfu Dajie, Chongwen District ☎ 6715 1687 🕐 Daily 9.30–5.30 🚇 Tiantandongmen 🚌 6, 35, 51, 60

---

### EXPORTING ANTIQUES

Chinese authorities classify any item made before 1949 as an antique. The export of any such item must be approved by the Beijing Cultural Relics Bureau, in the form of a red wax seal and an official receipt; any genuine antiques dealer should be able to show you this. The vast majority of "antiques" are really reproductions, so the need for export approval does not arise very often. If you buy an antique that lacks the seal, you can have it verified and approved at the Friendship Store (☎ 6500 3311 for an appointment) every Monday afternoon.

### SILK MARKET

The market, now indoors, is crammed with stands. Shoppers, mostly visitors and expatriates, but many Beijingers too, fill every space and at times the atmosphere can seem frenzied. Apart from silk and cashmere, available at phenomenally low prices, bargains are to be had in clothes, shoes and patchwork quilts. Famous brand names sit alongside impressive fakes and factory seconds.

🚇 M6/7 ✉ Xiushuidong Jie, Chaoyang District 🕐 Daily 10–dusk 🚇 Jianguomen

### TIANTAN PARK MARKET

A covered corridor near the park's east entrance is filled with stands displaying bric-a-brac and fascinating cultural curios from the 1960s. Look out for the ubiquitous Maoist clocks depicting revolutionary peasants holding aloft the Little Red Book.

🚇 J9 ✉ East side of Tiantan Park, Chongwen District 🕐 Daily 9–5.30 🚌 6, 15, 17, 20, 35, 39, 43, 106

### YUANLONG SILK CORPORATION LTD.

This is one of the oldest silk stores in Beijing, easy to find near the north entrance of Tiantan Park. A tailoring service is available.

🚇 H8 ✉ 55 Tiantan Lu, Chongwen District ☎ 6705 22451 🕐 Daily 9–5 🚌 34, 35, 36

# Entertainment and Nightlife

## CENTRO

Currently a very popular nightspot in the Kerry Centre (▷ 58), Centro is a giant cocktail bar and lounge with a private room and wine cellars. The happy hour and friendly waiters add to its appeal.

➕ Off map, east of M5
✉ 1st Floor, Kerry Centre Hotel, 1 Guanghua Lu, Chaoyang District ☎ 6561 8833 🕒 24 hours
🚇 Guomao 🚌 48, 908

## GOOSE & DUCK

A passable imitation of an English pub, with Bass ale from the barrel. Live music most nights.
➕ L6 ✉ 1 Bihuju Nanlu, Chaoyang District ☎ 6538 1691 🕒 24 hours
🚇 Dongsishitiao, then bus 115

## HUAXIA CULTURAL AND MARTIAL ARTS CENTER

Different groups perform here on different nights of the week. The Wushu, a fast performance of tai chi using swords, is especially popular.
➕ H5 ✉ National Children's Arts Theater, 64 Dong'anmen Dajie, Dongcheng District
☎ 6512 9687 🚌 103, 104

## LAO SHE TEAHOUSE

The Chinese cultural shows staged here nightly enliven excerpts from Chinese opera with comedy routines (in Chinese but highly visual). There are also martial arts,

acrobatics and magic.
➕ G7 ✉ 3rd Floor, Da Wan Cha Building, 3 Qianmenxi Dajie, Xuanwu District
☎ 6303 6830 🕒 Daily 7.30–9.30 🚇 Qianmen

## LIYUAN THEATER

The Beijing Opera Troupe performs Chinese opera here daily. Screens alongside the stage carry English translations, and English program notes help you to appreciate what is going on during the show as you sit at the Ming-style tables sipping tea.
➕ F8 ✉ Qianmen Hotel, 175 Yong'an Lu, Xuanwu District ☎ 6301 6688 ext. 8860 🕒 7.30–8.40 🚌 15, 23, 25, 102

---

### CHINESE OPERA

This highly stylized ancient art form has only a passing resemblance to Western opera and leaves most Westerners utterly bemused. The richly costumed players mix dance and song with mime—accompanied by Chinese instruments. Some grasp of the basic plot will help in understanding the action. The usual five-hour performance is reduced to a mere 90 minutes for the benefit of foreigners, although full performances are rare nowadays. The shortest performances are at the Lao She Teahouse.

---

## NATIONAL GRAND THEATER

This controversial new multistage venue, due to open in the second half of 2007, will host opera, theater and concert performances.
➕ F6 ✉ Xichang'an Jie
🚇 Tian'anmen Xi

## TIAN QIAO ACROBATICS THEATER

The well-known acrobatic and dance troupe performs in this 100-year-old theater.
➕ G9 ✉ 95 Tian Qiao Shichang Lu (east end of Beiwei Lu), Xuanwu District
☎ 6303 7449 🕒 Nightly performances 5.30–6.30, 7.15–8.40 🚌 59

## ZHENGYICI THEATER

The history of this theater goes back to 1620, when it was first built as a temple. Today, there is nowhere better to watch Beijing opera. During the day, the theater is a teahouse.
➕ F7 ✉ 220 Qianmen Xiheyan Dajie, Xuanwu District
☎ 6315 1649 🕒 Nightly performances 🚇 Hepingmen

# Restaurants

### PRICES

Prices are approximate, based on a 3-course meal for one person.

| | |
|---|---|
| YYY | over 250 yuan |
| YY | 100–250 yuan |
| Y | under 100 yuan |

### BEIJING AH YAT ABALONE RESTAURANT (YYY)

This restaurant is run by a chef who views Cantonese food as the pinnacle of Chinese cuisine. If you're really adventurous (and haven't tasted it in Hong Kong, where it is popular) try the edible bird's nest.

➕ Off map, east of M6 ✉ 1A Jianguomenwai Dajie, Chaoyang District ☎ 6508 9613 🕐 Daily 10.30–10.30 🚇 Guomao

### BIANYIFANG ROAST DUCK RESTAURANT (YY)

This famous roast duck restaurant has two dining areas, one pricier but also more pleasant, with more comfortable seats.

➕ J7 ✉ Hademen Hotel, 2c Chongwenmennai Dajie, Chongwen District ☎ 6712 0505 🕐 Daily lunch and dinner 🚇 Chongwenmen

### BLEU MARINE (YY–YYY)

This oh-so-French bistro with outdoor café-style seating serves up French countryside fare. The sandwiches are hearty and the wine list is reasonably extensive.

➕ M5 ✉ 5 Guanghua Xilu, Jianguomenwai embassy area, Chaoyang District ☎ 6500 6704 🕐 Daily 11.30–11.30 🚇 Yonganli

### LE CAFÉ IGOSSO (YY)

Currently one of the most popular Italian restaurants in the capital, Igosso's hallmarks are its relaxed, friendly atmosphere (children welcome), excellent risottos, delicious homemade bread and eminently affordable prices.

➕ Off map, east of M9 ✉ Dongsanhuannan Lu (0.5 miles/800m south of Guomao Bridge on east side of street), Chaoyang District ☎ 8771 7013 🕐 Daily 11.30am–1am 🚇 Guomao, then buses 28, 52

### NORTHERN CUISINE

This category of Chinese food—taking in the whole area north of the Yangtze—includes imperial cuisine (reserved, and specially prepared, for the court), Beijing duck and traditional city fare, along with food from remote northern areas like Mongolia and Dongbei. Instead of rice, noodles and steamed bread provide the basic sustenance, accompanied by vegetables and cold appetizers. Street cuisine is quickly cooked food from mobile stands with hotplates—pancakes filled with cooked vegetables are particularly delicious but it is wise to avoid meat fillings.

### DANIELI'S (YYY)

You will find Beijing's only homemade pasta served here and a marvelous range of sauces from tomato to carbonara. The salad is fresh and the wines are reasonably priced. It is also great to relax in the big, comfy chairs after a day's hard touring.

➕ M6 ✉ 2nd Floor, St. Regis Hotel, 21 Jianguomenwai Dajie, Jianguomenwai embassy area, Chaoyang District ☎ 6460 6688 ext. 2440 🕐 Daily 11.30–2.30, 6–10 🚇 Yonganli

### GONGDELIN (YY)

This is a branch of a famous Shanghai vegetarian restaurant, with its own delightful English-language menu featuring, for example, "the Fire is singeing the Snow-Capped Mountains." The food is excellent and the mock-meat dishes satisfy even the most steadfast meat-eaters.

➕ G8 ✉ 158 Qianmen Dajie, Chongwen District ☎ 6511 2542 🕐 Daily 10.30–8.30 🚇 Qianmen

### HATSUNE (YYY)

Perhaps the best recommendation for this award-winning Japanese restaurant is that it numbers visiting Tokyo businesspeople among its regular diners. The chef uses only the freshest ingredients in preparing the sushi, sashimi and tempura, all of which are

immaculately presented by attentive waitstaff.
🔟 Off map, east of M5
✉ 2nd Floor, Heqiao Building C, 8A Guanghua Lu (4 blocks east of Kerry Centre), Chaoyang District ☎ 6581 3939 🕐 Daily 11.30–2, 5.30–10 🚇 Guomao

### JUSTINE'S (YYY)
One of Beijing's most established Continental restaurants and an excellent choice for Sunday brunch. The main courses lean toward French cuisine but it's nothing fancy, just solid, consistent, moderately expensive Western food.
🔟 L5 ✉ 1st Floor, Jianguo Hotel, 5 Jianguomenwai Dajie, Chaoyang District ☎ 6500 2233 ext. 8039 🕐 Daily 12–2.30, 6–10.30 🚇 Yonganli

### KING ROAST DUCK (YY)
If you're aiming to eat Beijing duck every night while you are in Beijing, go here. Not only can you get the Imperial duck, but also sides of duck liver and lettuce-wrapped minced duck.
🔟 Off map, east of M6 ✉ 24 Jianguomenwai Dajie, Chaoyang District ☎ 6515 6908 🕐 Daily 10– 9.30 🚇 Yonganli 🚌 1, 4, 37, 52

### MEXICAN WAVE (YY)
Margaritas and beer imported from Mexico make an appropriate prelude to the pizzas, quesadillas, burritos, burgers and huge salads.

Near the corner of Guanghua Lu.
🔟 M5 ✉ Dongdaqiao Lu, Chaoyang District ☎ 6506 3961 🕐 Daily 10am–2am 🚇 Yonganli 🚌 28, 403

### QUANJUDE KAOYADIAN (YY–YYY)
The name means "old duck," but don't be put off–this is a fine place for a Beijing duck banquet. The restaurant has been in the same family since 1864 and is now the flagship for a group of restaurants including a take-out place next door. Be warned, service is leisurely to slow.
🔟 G7 ✉ 32 Qianmenxi Dajie, Chongwen District ☎ 6304 8987 🕐 Daily 11–1.30, 4.30–8 🚇 Qianmen

### RED CAPITAL (YYY)
Reserve a table here as soon as you arrive in

---

**BEIJING DUCK**

Slices of roast duck are placed inside a thin pancake along with onion or cucumber and sometimes sweetened with plum sauce or a wheat jam. The result is very rich and it's best not to think about the cholesterol count. A real feast begins with cold duck and ends with duck soup. A side plate of mashed garlic acts as an antidote to the rich, oily duck skin and meat.

---

Beijing. It's the place to go to impress guests. With a 1950s-style cigar and cocktail lounge and a lush courtyard setting, it's genuinely relaxing despite its Cultural Revolution nostalgia. Plus, the Beijing-style cooking is delightful and plentiful.
🔟 J3 ✉ 66 Dongsi Jiutiao, Dongcheng District ☎ 8401 6152 🕐 Dinner daily 🚇 Zhangzizhonglu

### STEAK AND EGGS (YY)
No-frills American cooking is the specialty of this popular diner tucked behind the Friendship Store. Head here for Sunday brunch—if you can find a table.
🔟 M6 ✉ 5 Xiushuinan Jie, Jianguomenwai, Chaoyang District ☎ 6592 8088 🕐 Mon–Fri 7.30am–10.30pm, Sat-Sun 7.30am–midnight 🚇 Jianguomen

### THE TAJ PAVILION (YY–YYY)
Excellent Indian food for vegetarians and meat-eaters. Service is friendly and the spinach or potato paneer are rich. Try their lassi drinks as well.
🔟 Off map, east of M6 ✉ 1st Floor, West Wing, China World Trade Centre, 1 Jianguomenwai Dajie, Chaoyang District ☎ 6505 2288 ext. 80116 🕐 Daily 11.30–2.30, 6–10.30 🚇 Guomao 🚌 1, 4, 37, 52

**Stretching generally northeast from the Forbidden City and Beihai Park, the Dongcheng district is speckled with parks, museums and temples, and still retains some of the traditional housing areas called *hutongs*.**

**I**

**2**

**3**

**4**

**5**

Qianxiaojie

Yongkang

Guoziji

Xiella   Hutong

Fensiting Hutong

ANDINGMENNEI   DAJIE

Beiluogu Xiang

Xiaoju'erchang Hutong

Xigong Jie

Dongong Jie

**GULOUDONG     DAJIE**

Qiangulouyuan Hutong

Ju'er  Hutong

DAJIE

Fangzhuanchang Hutong

Heizhima Hutong

Houyuan'ensi  Hutong

Nanluogu  Xiang

Shajing Hutong

Jingyang Hutong

Qinlao  Hutong

Taixin

Di'ANMENWAI    DAJIE

Mao'er

Hutong

Beibingmasi   Hutong

JIAODAOKOUNAN

Dongwar

Yu'er  Hutong

Dongmianhua   Hutong

Dongguanfang Hutong

Suoyi Hutong

Banchang  Hutong

**Wen Tianxiang Temple**

Fuxiang  Hutong

Chaodou  Hutong

**DI'ANMENDONG     DAJIE**

Beihe Hutong

Liboyi Hutor

Di'ANMENNEI  DAJIE

Congjian Hutong

Jie

Zhiranju   Hutong

Shubei Hutong

Jie

MEISHUGUANHOU

Shani Hutor

Xiyanw Hutong

Huanghuamen  Jie

Dongbanqiao

Jiansuozuo Xiang

Songzhuyuanbei  Xiang

Datoudong Jie

JINGSHANHOU   JIE

Sanyanjing Hutong

Donghuangchenggenbei

Xiaoqudeng Hutong

JINGSHANXI  JIE

**Children's Palace**

JINGSHANDONG  JIE

Shatanbei  Jie

Belheyan

**National Art Museum of China**

MEISHUGUANDONG

*Jingshan Park*

Shatanhou  Jie

Shatanbei Jie

Zhonglao Hutong

**WUSI     DAJIE**

**JINGSHANQIAN      JIE**

Cuihua Hutong

Beichizi

Tinchia Hutong

Qiheloubei  Xiang

Dajie

Donghuangchenggenan

Dongchang Hutong

Belheyan

Fuqiang  Hutong

Wangfujing

Qihelou  Jie

Dengshikouxi Jie

**F**            **G**            **H**

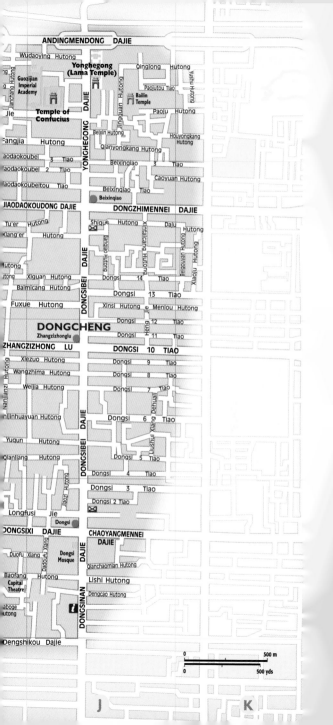

# Jingshan Park

*View of the Forbidden City from Jingshan Park (left); pink peony (right)*

## THE BASICS

+ G4
- ✉ Jingshanqian Xijie, Dongcheng District
- ☎ 6404 4071
- 🕐 Summer daily 5.30am–10.30pm; winter daily 6.30am–8pm
- 🚌 101, 103 or Tiananmen Xi then bus
- ♿ None
- 💰 Inexpensive

### DID YOU KNOW?

● Jingshan Park was not open to the public until 1928, and it was off limits again during the Cultural Revolution.
● In 1644, the last Ming emperor is said to have hanged himself from a tree in the park. The spot is signposted and marked by a tree (not the original).

**Get the best panoramic views of the Forbidden City's gold and russet roof-scape from the top of the Pavilion of Everlasting Spring. Come here before visiting the Forbidden City and you will understand its vast scale.**

**Coal Hill** As far back as the Yuan dynasty (1279–1368), Jingshan Park was the private recreational preserve for the imperial family. In the 15th century, when the moat for the Forbidden City was under construction, the demands of *feng shui* dovetailed with engineers' need to remove tons of earth. By using this to create large mounds to the north of the imperial palace, the royal residence was sited on high ground and thereby protected from malignant spirits. A story circulated that one emperor kept coal under one of the artificial hills. Coal Hill is another name for Jingshan Park.

**Vantage point** In addition to the compelling sight of the Forbidden City, the central pavilion—perched on the highest point in the park and easily reached from the park's main entrance—also takes in views of the long lake in Beihai Park and its White Dagoba (▷ 80). The perspective of the city as a whole reveals how remarkably flat most of Beijing is, and it is easy to imagine the force of the biting winter winds scudding across the city.

**Dance to the beat** Back at the bottom you may catch a glimpse of a troupe of players re-creating an imperial procession, with the "empress" in her sedan, to the sound of court music.

*Appreciating the art on display in the National Art Museum of China*

# National Art Museum of China

## THE BASICS

**www**.namoc.org

✚ H4

✉ 1 Wusi Dajie, Dongcheng District

☎ 6401 2252

🕐 Tue–Sun 9–4

🚌 103, 104, 108, 109, 111, 112

♿ None

💷 Inexpensive

**Housed in one of the first landmark buildings built after the 1949 Communist takeover, this is the city's major art gallery and China's national art museum (NAMOC). A varied and constantly changing program affords an insight into the contemporary Chinese art scene.**

**Showcase art** Construction began in 1958 and ended in 1962 on the building that houses this striking museum. It combines elements of traditional Chinese architecture—such as the multiple roofs with their yellow-glazed tiles and turned-up eaves—and a blocky appearance more in tune with Socialist Realism. The museum reopened in 2003 after an extensive refurbishment.

**International styles** Visiting exhibitions from around the world generally take place on the ground floor. Contemporary Chinese art is displayed on the two upper floors, and the space is divided between the permanent collection, which counts more than 70,000 pieces (only a small proportion of which are displayed at one time), and temporary exhibitions. There's no Socialist Realism here. Instead, the subject matter is Chinese life, especially genuine scenes of rural activity. The style is often pictorial, and may be Western-influenced, or more likely a combination of Chinese and Western influences. Among the highlights here are the large Chinese oil-painting landscapes, like scaled-ups versions of the traditional scroll paintings. Other art forms on show are calligraphy, poster art, sculpture and installations.

## HIGHLIGHTS

● Visiting exhibitions, often of major international shows
● National art exhibition of China: competition winners in contemporary Chinese art

## TIP

● Work is to begin in 2007 (or possibly 2008) on a new wing that will more than double the museum's size, and is due to be completed in 2011. Meanwhile there is likely to be some disruption to the main site as work proceeds.

**DONGCHENG**

**TOP 25**

# Lama Temple

● Maitreya Buddha in the Wanfu Pavilion
● Hall of Eternal Harmony
● Prayer wheel

**TIP**

● The English-speaking guides who wait for customers outside the Lama Temple need to be careful not to say anything that accurately describes the situation of Tibet within China, making their services of even less use than those of guides to other sites in the city .

**This is undoubtedly the liveliest functioning temple in Beijing—colorful and exciting, redolent of incense and as popular with worshipers as with tourists.**

**From palace to lamasery** Built in 1694, this was the residence of Yongzheng, a son of Emperor Kangxi, until 1723, when the son became the new emperor. Following imperial tradition, his former house was converted to a temple and in 1744 it became a lamasery—a monastery for Tibetan and Mongolian Buddhist monks. Closed down during the Cultural Revolution, but saved from destruction by deputy prime minister Zhou Enlai, the Lama Temple reopened in 1980 as a functioning monastery with monks from Mongolia. It has been suggested that the place is purely a public-relations exercise, designed to demonstrate how

*Detail of the carved archway at the entrance to the Hall of Eternal Harmony (far left); a Tibetan Dharma Wheel (middle); worshipers holding incense sticks and praying (right); a gold deity (bottom left); the Hall of Eternal Harmony and the gateway to Lama Temple (bottom middle); a Buddhist monk (bottom right)*

the Chinese state tolerates Tibetan Buddhism. It has lovely gardens and a wonderful interior.

**Layout** The temple is a complex of halls and courtyards with a variety of interesting pavilions on either side. In the Hall of Celestial Kings, giant guardians flank a smiling Buddha. The next hall, the Hall of Eternal Harmony, has three Buddhas accompanied by 18 disciples. Beyond the next courtyard lie the Hall of Eternal Protection and the Hall of the Wheel of Law (the cycle of death and rebirth). The final hall, the Wanfu Pavilion, contains a 75ft-high (23m) buddha, carved in the mid-18th century from a single sandalwood tree from Tibet. A wonderful figure of a god with at least 30 hands is the focus of the Esoteric Hall on the temple's east side. One of two halls with the same name, it was used for the study of scriptures.

**THE BASICS**

✚ J1
✉ Yonghegong Dajie, Beixinqia, Dongcheng District
☎ 6404 4499
🕐 Daily 9–4.30
🚇 Yonghegong
🚌 13, 62, 116
♿ Inexpensive

# Temple of Confucius

## HIGHLIGHTS

● 700-year-old cypress tree
● Hall of Great Achievements
● Steles in the courtyard

## TIP

● Beijing's *hutongs*–old residential districts–have been disappearing for years to make way for modern developments, so take some time out to stroll through the *hutong* around the Temple of Confucius.

**Seek out this temple down an ancient *hutong*. Cooling cypresses in the courtyard lead to the tranquil temple with its commemorative arches over the doorway.**

**Confucius says** This noted philosopher and teacher (551–479BC) taught the virtues of moderation, family piety and nobility of mind through good behavior. His conservative belief in the natural hierarchy of the ruler and subject won him the favor of the emperors and, despite fierce criticism from the Communist Party, the influence of Confucius is still felt in Chinese society today.

**Outside the temple** Occupying the forecourt area are a number of cypress trees, including an ancient one supposedly planted when the temple was built in the 14th century. The other notable

*Red votives (left); exterior of the former Imperial College (middle); statue of Confucius (right); the 700-year-old cypress tree (bottom far left); stone relief on the steps (bottom left); inside the temple (bottom middle); incense sticks (bottom right)*

DONGCHENG

TOP 25

feature is a collection of steles that record the names of candidates who, between 1416 and 1904, successfully passed the notoriously severe civil service examinations. Adjoining the temple stands the Imperial College, now called the Capital Library, where the emperor would deliver his annual lecture on classic Confucian texts.

**Inside** The Temple of Confucius, built in 1302 and restored in 1411, does not contain any statues of the philosopher himself, but in the Hall of Great Achievements, the central altar contains a small wooden tablet dedicated to his memory. Emperors and high-ranking scholars came here to make offerings to the spirit of Confucius and conduct ancient rituals. Part of the temple is now the Capital Museum, housing an array of ritual implements used in the temple ceremonies.

THE BASICS

- J1
- Guozijian Jie, Dongcheng District
- 8401 1977
- Daily 8.30–5
- Yonghegong
- 13, 113, 104, 108
- None
- Inexpensive

71

# The Back Lakes and Parks

A bicycle tour allows you to experience an essential aspect of Beijing life. You can rent a bicycle at many hotels. Always use bicycle lanes.

**DISTANCE:** 8 miles (13km)    **ALLOW:** 3–4 hours (including visits)

**START**

**WANGFUJING DAJIE, AT DONG'ANMEN DAJIE**
🚫 H5 🚇 Dengshikou

❶ Head south down the car-free segment of Wangfujing Dajie and turn left at the vast Oriental Plaza mall into Dongchang'an Jie and left again into Dongdanbei Dajie.

❷ Ride north up this road for 2.5 miles (4km)—along the way its name changes to Dongsinan Dajie, Dongsibei Dajie and Yonghegong Dajie—to the Lama Temple (▷ 68–69).

❸ The temple is at the junction with Andingmendong Dajie (the Second Ring Road). Backtrack to the first street on the right, Guozijian Jie, which leads west past the Temple of Confucius (▷ 70–71) and the Imperial Academy.

❹ Continue to the T-junction with Andingmennei Dajie. Turn left and at the traffic lights turn right into Guloudong Dajie, continuing to a junction by the large red building, the Drum Tower (▷ 84).

**END**

**WANGFUJING DAJIE, AT DONG'ANMEN DAJIE**

❽ Go left into Jingshanqian Jie and, after passing the National Art Museum of China (▷ 67), turn right, to return to Wangfujing Dajie.

❼ Turn left into Di'Anmenxi Dajie and at the first junction with traffic lights go right into Di'Anmennei Dajie. Ride south to the T-junction at the edge of Jingshan Park (▷ 66). Turn left into Jingshanhou Jie and follow the street around the park (there's an entrance to your right) to another T-junction.

❻ A few hundred yards (meters) after a McDonald's restaurant, turn right into a lane, immediately after a bridge. Follow the lane to Qianhai Lake and keep the water to your right as far down as Di'Anmenxi Dajie.

❺ Turn left here into Di'Anmenwai Dajie.

# Shopping

### BEIJING FINE JEWELERS

Sanlitun outlet with great selection of gold, silver and other jewelry. If you have a favorite bangle, bring a photo of it and they will reproduce it.
🚇 M3 ✉ 6A Gongrentiyuchangdong Lu (aka Gongti Dong Lu), Chaoyang District ☎ 6592 7118 🕐 Daily 9.30–7 🚌 115, 118

### BEIJING GONG MEI ART WORLD

This huge emporium, conveniently situated on Beijing's main shopping street, is famous for its jade, but you'll also find gold and silver jewelry, glassware, carvings, cloisonné, lacquer, art materials and seals.
🚇 H5 ✉ 200 Wangfujing Dajie, Dongcheng District ☎ 6528 8866 🕐 Daily 9–9 🚇 Wangfujing 🚌 103, 104

### CHAOWAI MARKET

Two large warehouses at the end of a small lane are stuffed with antique objects of desire: medicine cabinets, first-class reproductions of Qing and Ming furniture, ceramics, Mao memorabilia, jewelry and other knickknacks. Packing and shipping are easily arranged. Serious bargaining is essential.
🚇 L4 ✉ Shichangie, Chaoyangmenwai Dajie, Chaoyang District 🕐 Daily 9–6 🚇 Chaoyangmen

### FOREIGN LANGUAGES BOOKSTORE

The largest stock of foreign-language books in the city. As well as books and tapes, dictionaries and other reference material is available in the Foreign Language Reference Bookstore at No. 219 Wangfujing.
🚇 H5 ✉ 235 Wangfujing Dajie, Dongcheng District ☎ 6512 6903 🕐 Daily 9–9 🚇 Wangfujing 🚌 104, 211

### LUFTHANSA CENTER

The fifth floor of this large shopping plaza is devoted to arts and crafts. A separate room serves as a gallery for Chinese prints. There's also one of Beijing's best super-markets.
🚇 Off map, east of M1 ✉ 50 Liangmaqiao Lu, Chaoyang District ☎ 6465

3388 🕐 Daily 9–9 🚌 300, 402, 801

### SANLITUN LU

Silk Market is the best-known place for designer clothes, but Sanlitun Lu may well prove equally rewarding. As the stands are mainly on one side of Sanlitunbeijielu, there is more space for walking, looking and trying on. Less hectic than the Silk Market, better prices can often be negotiated. The bulk of the merchandise consists of designer jeans, shirts and women's wear. There's a fruit and vegetable market around the corner.
🚇 Off map, east of M2 ✉ Off Sanlitun Lu, Chaoyang District 🕐 Daily 9–7 🚌 115, 118

### YONGHEGONG DAJIE

This row of shops on the way to the Lama Temple specialize in Buddhist religious paraphernalia—candles, incense sticks, statuettes, shrines, prayer cushions, prayer wheels.
🚇 J1 ✉ Yonghegong Dajie, Chaoyang District 🕐 Daily 8–7 🚇 Yonghegong

### XINDE CHINESE CLOTHING STORE

This fabulous clothes store specializes in reproducing Chinese fashions of the prerevolutionary era. Everything you see here is hand sewn.
🚇 G2 ✉ 108 Gulou Dongdajie, Dongcheng District ☎ 6402 6769 🕐 Daily 9–6 🚇 Guloudajie

# Entertainment and Nightlife

## CD CAFÉ JAZZ CLUB

The archetypal jazz club, smoky and dim, where you can relax and observe the city from an outdoor patio. Live music takes place from Wednesday to Sunday (small cover charge).
🚇 Off map, east of M2
✉ Dongsanhuanbei Lu, Chaoyang District (southwest of Museum of Agriculture)
☎ 6506 8288 🕐 Daily 4pm–2am 🚌 300, 402, 801

## CHAMPAGNE BAR

One of the better hotel bars in Beijing. The resident band, typically Filipino, jump-starts the evening around 7.30, after happy hour, and continues until 1am. Reservations are available.
🚇 Off map, east of M4
✉ Jing Guang Centre, Dongsanhuanbei Lu, Chaoyang District ☎ 6597 8888 ext. 2561 🕐 Daily 4pm–1am 🚌 112, 113, 9, 402

## CHINA ACROBATIC TROUPE

This remarkable troupe, founded over 40 years ago, offers one of Beijing's more enjoyable evening experiences. The repertoire encompasses plate stacking and spinning, tightrope walking, magic and juggling, interspersed with breathtaking gymnastic displays that are often packed with dramatic surprises involving bicycles or pieces of furniture. Highly recommended.

🚇 Off map, east of M4
✉ Chaoyang Theater, 36 Dongsanhuan Beilu, Chaoyang District (opposite Jing Guang Hotel) ☎ 6507 2421/1818 🕐 Daily 7.15pm 🚌 9, 113, 402, 405, 801

## CLUB FOOTBALL CENTER

Inside the Red House Hotel, this bar has a real pub atmosphere, at least when they're screening British and European soccer matches, or NBA (US basketball) and NFL (US football) games. Work off those extra calories playing pool, table football or darts. Food available.
🚇 L3 ✉ 10 Chunxiu Lu, Chaoyang District ☎ 6416 7786 🕐 Daily 11am–midnight 🚇 Dongsishitiao 🚌 117

## CLUB LOOK

The latest nightspot from the Henry Lee stable is a huge affair comprising a dining room and two bars, where the resident DJs play mainly hip hop.
🚇 N4 ✉ Gongrentiyuchang

### FAST-CHANGING SCENE

Informal restaurants during the day and early evening, Beijing's licensed cafés gradually transform themselves into bars as the night goes on. Always call before heading off for the night–don't forget to ask your hotel to write down the name and address in Chinese for the benefit of taxi drivers.

Beilu (aka Gongti Beilu, first *hutong* on the right after Sanlitun Lu), Chaoyang District ☎ 6506 6770 🕐 Daily 8.30pm–late 🚌 115, 118

## COCO CLUB

Latin American music and food sets the scene in this comfortable hotel bar. Early in the evening you can enjoy a game of darts or a quiet conversation, but when the band starts up, just sit back and enjoy the show.
🚇 H5 ✉ Prime Hotel, 2 Wangfujing Dajie, Dongcheng District ☎ 6513 6666 🕐 Daily 6pm–1.30am 🚌 104, 111

## DURTY NELLIE'S

This Irish pub, where Guinness is on tap, is a favorite hangout for locals and expatriates. Soups, sandwiches, salads and more are available. Cover bands often play modern pop and rock music.
🚇 Off map, east of M1
✉ 8 Dongshanhuan Beilu, Chaoyang District ☎ 6593 5050 🕐 Daily 5.30pm–1.30am 🚌 300, 402, 801

## EXPERIMENTAL THEATER FOR MODERN DRAMA

It is only since the death of Mao's fourth wife, an actress and the notorious leader of the Gang of Four, that the authorities have encouraged non-Chinese forms of theater. This is the main venue for such endeavors, and while some shows are

in Chinese, international groups also perform in English.

🕀 G/H3 ✉ 45A Mao'er Hutong, Xicheng District
☎ 6403 1009/6402 0151
🕐 Evenings 🚌 5, 107, 305

### FRANK'S PLACE AT TRIO

This bar in the Lido area, west of the Rosedale Hotel, remains a firm favorite with regulars. It's a good place to catch an international sports event on television.

🕀 Off map, northeast of M1
✉ Jiangtai Xilu, Chaoyang District ☎ 6437 8399
🕐 Daily 11.30am–1.30am
🚌 359, 401, 403, 404

### HARD ROCK CAFÉ

Rock memorabilia, pricey drinks and tasty barbecued pork chops and grilled fajitas. A resident band plays short sessions after 9pm, except Sunday, when there is a disco (cover charge).

🕀 Off map, east of M2 ✉ 8 Dongsanhuan Beilu, Chaoyang District (next to Great Wall Sheraton Hotel) ☎ 6590 6688 🕐 Sun–Thu 11.30pm–2am (3am at weekends) 🚌 300, 402, 801

### JAZZ YA

One of the best cocktail menus in this part of town draws local yuppies and expatriates from around the globe. The food is Western, while the jazz is international.

🕀 Off map, east of M2

✉ 18 Sanlitun Beilu, Chaoyang District ☎ 6415 1227 🕐 Daily 10.30am–2am
🚌 115, 118

### NIGHTMAN CLUB

Only a few years ago, dance clubs were unknown in China, so although the Nightman may seem a little unsophisticated, it is still remarkable how exuberantly Beijingers have warmed to the genre.

🕀 Off map, north of M1
✉ 2 Xibahenan Lu (opposite west gate of International Exhibition Center), Chaoyang District ☎ 6461 5629
🕐 Daily 8.30pm–5am
🚌 302, 379, 18

### POLY PLAZA INTERNATIONAL THEATER

This is a major venue for ballet, music and opera—Puccini's *Turandot*, the New York City Ballet or the Beijing Jazz Festival.

---

#### BAR HOPPING

The Sanlitun Lu area is the only part of Beijing where you can bar-hop on foot. In addition to the establishments mentioned on these pages, there are a host of other places in the vicinity. The small *hutongs* between Gongrentiyuchangdong Lu and Nansanlitun Lu (🕀 M4) are alight with neon at night and more bars cluster behind the Swing bar at No. 58 farther up Sanlitun Lu.

---

🕀 L2 ✉ 14 Dongzhimennan Dajie, Dongcheng District
☎ 6500 1188 ext. 5126
🚇 Dongsishitiao

### PUBLIC SPACE

With its air of relaxed informality and tables on the sidewalk, this typical Sanlitun bar is buoyantly decorated and stays open until dawn if demand warrants.

🕀 M2 ✉ 50 Sanlitun Beilu, Chaoyang District ☎ 6416 0759 🕐 Daily 10am–2am
🚌 115, 18

### THE TREE

Formerly The Hidden Tree (at a different location), this café accompanies a roster of Belgian beers—among them refreshing Hoegaarden *witbier* and Antwerp's De Koninck beer—with wood-fired pizzas and other Mediterranean munchies.

🕀 M2 ✉ 43 Beisanlitun Nanlu, Chaoyang District
☎ 6415 1594 🕐 Daily 11am–4am 🚌 18, 115

### WAITING FOR GODOT

A literary café that is the brainchild of Zhao Liao, a Beijing intellectual with a passion for the theater. Sip a coffee or choose a quirky beer while looking over the collection of unusual CDs and art books.

🕀 H2 ✉ 24 Building 14 Jiaodaokou Dongdajie, Xicheng District ☎ 6407 3093
🕐 Daily 10am–2am
🚇 Beixingqiao

# Restaurants

## PRICES

Prices are approximate,
based on a 3-course
meal for one person.

| | |
|---|---|
| YYY | over 250 yuan |
| YY | 100–250 yuan |
| Y | under 100 yuan |

### AFUNTI (YY)
Roasted lamb or chicken
with nan bread are favor-
ites at this Muslim Uighur
restaurant. Ethnic music
and dancing in the
evening make for an
enjoyable night out.
⊞ K4 ⊠ 2a Houguaibang
Hutong, Chaoyang mennei
Dajie, Chaoyang District
☎ 6527 2288 ⏰ Daily 11am
until the last customers leave
🚌 101, 110, 202

### ASIAN STAR (YY)
Eclectic menu with Thai,
Malaysian and Indonesian
fare as well as a host of
Indian dishes. Options
such as curries and
tandoori chicken vie
with the Malaysian
dishes as some of the
best Asian eating you will
find in Beijing.
⊞ Off map, east of M3
⊠ 26 Dongsanhuanbei Lu,
Chaoyang District ☎ 6582
5306 ⏰ Daily 11–2.30,
5–10.30 🚌 113, 402, 405

### BA GUO BU YI (YY)
The decor in this Sichuan-
ese restaurant is reminiscent of a Qing dynasty
inn. The extensive
English-language picture
menu ranges from *mapo
dofu* (braised chicken

with dried bamboo
shoots) to more exotic
dishes like sharks' lips
and bullfrog.
⊞ G3 ⊠ 89 Di'anmen
Dongdajie, Dongcheng District
☎ 6400 8888 ⏰ Daily
11.15–2.30, 5–9.30 🚌 13, 42,
58, 60

### DING TAI ZHEN (Y)
The large menu in English
includes many fish dishes
and unusual appetizers
like lotus root. This
licensed restaurant is
suitable for vegetarians.
Try the Iron Fairy tea.
⊞ J4 ⊠ 116 Dongsinan
Dajie, Chaoyang District
☎ 6522 7286 ⏰ Daily
10–10 🚇 Dongsi 🚌 110,
116, 120, 204

### THE MIDDLE 8TH
### RESTAURANT (YY)
Sample the subtle
delights of Yunnanese
cooking, its scents and
aromas reminiscent of

## DINING WITH A VIEW

On the 26th floor of the
Xiyuan Hotel, the Carousel
revolving restaurant serves
Beijing and other Asian dishes while taking in panoramic
views of the city. The TV
Tower has a restaurant and
café, but its view cannot
match that of the Belle Vue
restaurant on the 29th floor
at the Kunlun Hotel (⊞ N2
opposite the Lufthansa
Center), which takes about
90 minutes to complete
one revolution.

Thai cuisine, before hot-
footing it to Sanlitun for
a nightcap.
⊞ Off map, east of M2
⊠ Sanlitun Zhongba Lu,
Chaoyang District ☎ 6413
0629 ⏰ Daily 11–2, 5–10.30
🚌 113, 117

### PASS BY BAR (YY)
At the Guloudong Dajie
end of Nanluogu Xiang,
Beijing's classiest bar and
restaurant street, Pass By
is a great place to relax
after a day's sightseeing.
Sit back and enjoy a
pizza, a plate of pasta or
a US-imported Angus sir-
loin, accompanied by the
Californian house wine.
There's courtyard dining
in summer.
⊞ H2 ⊠ 108 Nanluogu
Xiang, Dongcheng District
☎ 8403 8004 ⏰ Daily
9pm–2am 🚌 18, 204

### SERVE THE PEOPLE
### (Y–YY)
It's trendy and serves reasonably priced Thai food.
⊞ M3 ⊠ 1 Xiwujie Sanlitun,
Chaoyang District ☎ 8454
4580 ⏰ Daily 10.30–10.30
🚌 115, 118

### THE TANDOOR (YYY)
This restaurant has an
established reputation
for top-notch north
Indian cooking.
⊞ Off map, east of M3
⊠ 1st Floor, Great Dragon
Hotel, 2 Gongrentiyuchangbei
Lu, Chaoyang District
☎ 6597 2211/2299 ext. 2112
⏰ Daily 11.30–2, 5.30–10.30
🚌 113, 208

Beihai Park, a former imperial park that is now a part of the people's Beijing, is the highlight of a district that stretches northwest from the Forbidden City out to another green area, Beijing Zoo.

# Beihai Park

## HIGHLIGHTS

● The White Dagoba on Jade Island
● Elaborate, imperial-style Fangshan restaurant (▷ 89)
● Dragon Screen, on the north shore of the lake
● 17th-century Five Dragon Pavilions, near Dragon Screen
● Kublai Khan's jade vase, the largest of its kind in China

**Kublai Khan is reputed to have created this popular park, the largest in Beijing. Half water and half land, it offers a placid charm and an opportunity to relax in the heart of the city, so long as you avoid visiting on a weekend.**

Imperial landscape  The lake in the park was dug during the Jin dynasty (12th–13th century), before the Forbidden City was thought of. All that remains of Kublai Khan's presence now is a large, decorated jade vessel that was presented to him in 1265. It is on show in the Round City, inside the south entrance to the park on Wenjin Jie. During the Qing dynasty, Emperor Qianlong (1736–95) directed an ambitious landscaping project that laid the foundations for an exemplary Chinese classical garden. Jiang Qing, widow of Mao Zedong and a

*The White Dagoba on Jade Island (far left); a white jade Buddha statue in the Hall of Receiving Light (middle); Dragon Screen (right); Beihai Park, Sazhou Village (bottom left); The Hall of Receiving Light (bottom middle); people strolling through the park (bottom right)*

20th-century empress of sorts, visited regularly in the 1980s.

**Stroll, row and sightsee** Inside the south gate is the Round City consisting of a pavilion and court-yard. Beyond, the Hall of Receiving Light was originally a superior gatepost house for emperors and now contains a Buddha crafted from white jade, a present from Burma to Empress Dowager Cixi, who ruled from 1861 to 1908. From the hall, the way leads to a short walk across the lake to Jade Island, noted for the White Dagoba, a 130ft-high (36m) Buddhist shrine constructed in 1651 for a visit to Beijing by the Dalai Lama. Also here is the famous Fangshan restaurant, serving favorite imperial dishes, and a dock where you can rent rowboats. Locals crowd here on the weekends for family picnics and romantic getaways.

**THE BASICS**

www.beihaipark.com.cn
✚ F3–F4
✉ Wenjin Jie, Xicheng District
☎ 6403 3225
🕐 Park daily 7am–8pm; sights 9–4.45
🍴 Snack and drink shops; Fangshan restaurant
🚌 13, 101, 103, 107, 109, 111 or 5 from Tiananmen Xi subway
♿ None
💰 Inexpensive

# Beijing's *Hutongs*

### HIGHLIGHTS

Areas with old or especially well-preserved *hutongs*:
● Drum and Bell Towers
● Qianhai-Houhai
● North and south of Fuchengmennei Dajie
● Nanluoguxiang and around
● West of the Temple of Confucius

**Stroll through these centuries-old alley-ways, dotted about with mansions, for a fascinating insight into a communal lifestyle that is fast disappearing.**

**Origins** The word *hutong* dates back to the Yuan dynasty (13th century) and is derived from the Mongolian for "well," the traditional focal point of the village. By 1949 there were nearly 6,000 of these rambling lanes, and their names often reveal something intriguing about their past, for example, *liulichang* (tilemakers' alley) or *lurou* (donkey-meat alley). Some are truly labyrinthine, with as many as 20 turns, while others are tiny—only 11 yards (10m) long and 15.5in (40cm) wide.

**Prince Gong's Residence** During the Ming and Qing dynasties, imposing residences called

*Communal living (left), together with the jumble of rooftops (middle and bottom left) and narrow alleyways (right and bottom right) are features of hutongs*

*siheyuan* (literally meaning "four-sided courtyard") were built between the *hutongs* for merchants, wealthy noblemen or high-ranking officials. Prince Gong's Residence is a typical example. It dates from 1777 and was restored in 2006. The main attraction for foreign visitors is the traditional Chinese garden, complete with rock gardens and water courses.

**The future** The future of *hutongs* and *siheyuan* is uncertain as the battle rages between the forces of preservation on the one hand, and the forces of progress on the other. Some courtyard houses have been preserved as cultural monuments, while others are being restored and adapted for private or commercial use. While many residents complain about unsanitary living conditions, others value the sense of community.

## THE BASICS

**Prince Gong's Residence**

➕ F2

✉ 14 Liuyin Jie/Qianhai Xijie, Xicheng District

☎ 6616 8149

🕐 Daily 8.30–4.30

🍴 Sichuan Fandian restaurant on Liuyin Jie

🚌 107, 111, 118

💷 Inexpensive

❓ Guided tours available from entrance

# More to See

## ANCIENT CURRENCY MUSEUM

On the site of the Zhen Wu Museum, a building from the Qing dynasty, this museum displays currency ranging from seashells used in ancient times to the renminbi used today. There are more than 2,000 different pieces of currency exhibited ranging from shells to stone, jade, bone, gold and copper.

➕ E1 ✉ Deshengmen Jianlu, Xicheng District, North 2nd Ring ☎ 6201 8073 🕐 Tue–Sun 9–4 🚇 Jishuitan ♿ None 💷 Inexpensive

## BEIJING AQUARIUM

Adjacent to Beijing Zoo, this large aquarium concentrates on regional marine life. The shark tank and killer whale (orca) show are must-sees.

➕ A1 ✉ 137 Xizhimenwai, Xicheng District ☎ 6217 6655 🕐 Daily 9–5.30 (Jun–Sep 9–6) 🚇 Xizhimen ♿ None 💷 Expensive

## BEIJING ZOO

Depressing by the standards of its best Western counterparts, Beijing Zoo is worthwhile for its famous giant panda house. Spare a moment for the lesser panda from Sichuan province. Tucked away in the northwest of the city, the zoo is easily reached by subway but avoid weekends, when it is particularly busy.

➕ A2 ✉ 137 Xizhimenwai Dajie, Xicheng District ☎ 6831 4411 🕐 Summer daily 7.30–6; winter 8–5 🚇 Xizhimen ♿ None 💷 Inexpensive

## BELL AND DRUM TOWERS

These massive structures were Beijing's timekeepers for more than 600 years. The Zhonglu (Bell Tower) dates from the Yuan dynasty and was last rebuilt in 1747, in brick and stone. Prepare for a tough climb to the gallery on the second floor. The bronze bell, cast during the Ming dynasty, is the largest in China, and can be heard up to 12 miles (20km) away. The Gulou (Drum Tower) was rebuilt at the same time as the Bell Tower and houses 24 drums, one for each hour of the day, though only the battered one with the torn ox-hide skin is original.

➕ G2 ✉ 9 Zhonggulou Dajie/Di'anmen

The Bell Tower

Beijing Aquarium

Dajie ☎ 6401 2674 ⏰ Daily 9–5. Drum-beating ceremony in Drum Tower every half hour 9–11.30, 1–5.30 🍴 Café opposite Bell Tower 🚇 Guloudajie, then follow signs 👊 Moderate

### FIVE-PAGODA TEMPLE
Established in the 15th century, this little-visited Indian-style temple and its adjoining Museum of Stone Carvings are well worth combining with a trip to the zoo (▷ 84). The temple's pagodas are covered with exquisite Buddhist bas-reliefs; climb the stair-way for a closer view.
✚ A1 ✉ 24 Wutasicun, Haidian District ☎ 6217 3836 ⏰ Daily 8.30–4.30 🚇 Xizhimen 👊 Inexpensive

### FORMER RESIDENCE OF SOONG QING-LING
Soong Qing-Ling, the wife of Sun Yat Sen, the revolutionary leader, lived in this former Qing mansion—home to the father of China's last emperor—from 1963 until her death in 1981. Quite apart from the exhibits relating to her life, the gardens are exquisite

and worth a visit.
✚ F1 ✉ 46 Houhaibeiyan, Xicheng District ☎ 6404 4205 ⏰ Tue–Sat 9–5 🚌 5, 55 ⛔ None 👊 Inexpensive

### WHITE PAGODA TEMPLE
It is not easy to miss this 150ft-high (45m) pagoda, the largest in Beijing, built in the 13th century as a show-piece of the new Mongol capital. The Nepalese influence in its construction is still apparent. The pagoda is officially known as the Temple of the Miraculous Response.
✚ D3 ✉ Fuchengmennei Dajie, Xicheng District ☎ 6616 0211 ⏰ Daily 9–4.30 🚇 Fuchengmen ⛔ None 👊 Inexpensive

### XU BEIHONG MEMORIAL HALL
Xu Beihong (1895–1953) is China's foremost modern artist. The galleries display many of his paintings, includ-ing those of galloping horses for which he is most famous. Reproductions are on sale in the museum store.
✚ E1 ✉ 53 Xinjiekoubei Dajie, Xicheng District ☎ 6225 2265 ⏰ Daily 9–4 🚇 Jishuitan ⛔ None 👊 Inexpensive

*The Bell Tower's bronze bell*

*A red drum in the Drum Tower*

# Off the Tourist Trail

This walk shows workaday life for ordinary Beijingers and affords an opportunity to visit several lesser-known places of interest.

**DISTANCE:** 2.8 miles (4.5km) **ALLOW:** 3–4 hours, including sights

START

**FUCHENGMENNEI DAJIE**
➕ C4 🚇 Fuchengmen

END

**FUCHENGMENNEI DAJIE**

**1** From Fuchengmen metro station, walk the short distance to Fuchengmennei Dajie. Cross the street and turn right into Gongmenkoutou Tiao, in a *hutong* district speckled with shoe vendors and cobblers.

**2** Take the first street on the left, Fuchengmennei Beijie, which leads two blocks north to the Lu Xun Museum. The museum contains material related to the life of the progressive writer Lu Xun (1881–1936).

**3** Leaving the museum, backtrack to Fuchengmennei Dajie and go left (east) along this mixed residential and shopping street for two blocks.

**4** Turn left into Baitasidong Jadao, which leads to the White Pagoda Temple (▷ 85). This Buddhist temple's refurbished, tall, white stupa, is easily visible from around the *hutong* district.

**8** Alternatively, explore some of the *hutong* alleys on either side of Xi'anmen Dajie and Fuchengmennei Dajie before taking bus 42, 101, 102 or 103 back to the metro station.

**7** Keep going east on Fuchengmennei Dajie. Just before Xisi Beidajie is the Buddhist Guangji Temple, its main hall at the end of a tree-bordered courtyard. Outside the temple, go south for one block on Xisinan Dajie then right into Xi'anmen Dajie. Continuing eastward on this street brings you to Beihai Park (▷ 80–81).

**6** Cross over the busy intersection at Zhaodengyu Lu, to the restored 16th-century Temple of Ancient Monarchs (Lidai Diwang Miao), where the Ming and Qing emperors went to honor their predecessors.

**5** After visiting the temple, return to Fuchengmennei Dajie. Go left again.

# Shopping

## 77TH STREET PLAZA

This Singapore-based chain store retails youth-oriented fashion clothes and accessories with Asian style and street credibility for both boys and girls.

⊞ E5 ☒ Xidan Cultural Plaza, 180 Xidanbei Dajie, Xicheng District ☎ 6608 7177 ⏰ Daily 9.30am–10pm ⊜ Lingjing Hutong

## CARREFOUR

French-based international hypermarket selling, among other things, Western groceries and household items at reasonable prices.

⊞ Off map, north of A1 ☒ Zhongguancun Plaza, Haidian District ☎ 5172 1516 ⏰ Daily 9am–10pm ⊟ 320, 322

## GANJIAKOU

This market attracts few tourists because the clothes are entirely Asian in style, but it will appeal to those interested in investigating the latest fashions from Taiwan and Korea. Stands line the street, Sanlihe Lu, as far as Baiwanzhuangxi Lu. As usual in this type of market, bargaining is essential.

⊞ A3 ☒ Sanlihe Lu, Haidian District ⏰ Daily 9–5 ⊟ 102, 103, 114

## SCROLL ALLEY

Although way off the beaten track, this motley street market is easy to reach by subway. Walk east from Chegong-zhuang station, turning north when you see the stands on your left. A good place to have pictures mounted as scrolls.

⊞ C2 ☒ North of Ping'anlixi Dajie ⏰ Daily 9–5 ⊜ Chegongzhuang

## TIANYI MARKET

Not everyone who goes shopping in Beijing is looking to buy an imitation—or even a genuine—Ming dynasty vase. To shop where the ordinary folks do, there's nowhere better than this market that used to be a street market but, which like several others, has been banished indoors to a modern multistory building. This hasn't affected the sales of sports gear of all kinds, toys, clothes, household appliances and all kinds of knick-knacks. China's vast range of Christmas goods produced mainly for export finds a home here come December.

⊞ B4 ☒ Fuchengmenwai Dajie, Xicheng District ☎ 6831 7199 ⏰ Daily 7.30–5.30 ⊜ Fuchengmen

## XIDAN

The main thoroughfare that runs straight across the city from east to west changes its name four times and as Xichang'an Jie runs west from Tian'anmen Square before changing its name again to Fuxingmennei Dajie at Xidan. The Xidan area is worth exploring for its atmosphere, especially in the evening when lively street stands mushroom and crowds of Beijingers frantically shop for everyday household items.

⊞ E5–E6 ☒ Niu Jie, Xuanwu District ⏰ Daily 9am–10pm ⊜ Xidan

## ZHONGGUANCUN

Computer stores are concentrated here in the northwest of the city. (From Xizhimen subway station take a minibus along Baishiqiao Lu.) You will see the stores a couple of stops past the Friendship Hotel. A wide range of hardware, peripherals and software (beware—much of it is pirated) is available.

⊞ Off map, north of A1 ☒ Haidian Jie, Haidian District ⏰ Daily 9–5 ⊟ 301, 303, 332, 333

---

### BARGAINING

In Sanlitun and the Silk Market, and markets in general, there are no fixed prices and bargaining is the rule. In general, try to bring down the vendor's first asking price before committing yourself to an offer and remember that you will always need to settle at a price above your first offer. A pair of Armani jeans should go for around 100 yuan, Caterpillar boots or a Gore-Tex jacket for around twice that.

# Entertainment and Nightlife

## 13 CLUB

Students—both Chinese and international—are the main clientele at this sparely decorated, smoky, music and dance club. Beer flows in dirt-cheap abundance, and what the local bands may lack in polish they make up for in decibels.

🔼 Off map, north of A1
✉ 161 Lanqiying, Chengfu Lu, Haidian District ☎ 6088 7715
◉ Daily 6pm–2 or 3am
🚇 Wudaokou 🚌 320, 332

## BEIJING CONCERT HALL

There is nowhere better to appreciate classical Chinese music than in the 1,000-seat Beijing Concert Hall (Beijing Yinyueting), known for its excellent acoustics. Western music is also performed.

🔼 E6 ✉ 1 Beixinhua Jie, Xicheng District ☎ 6605 5812
◉ Evenings 🚇 Xidan

## EAST SHORE LIVE JAZZ CAFÉ

This jazz café's signature is straight-on, no-nonsense jazz played for an appreciative audience.

🔼 G2 ✉ 2 Qianhai Nanyan, Xicheng District ☎ 8403 2131
◉ Daily 11am–2am 🚌 58, 204, 306

## GUANGFUGUAN GREENHOUSE

This unpretentious bar on a restored Ming dynasty street just a stone's throw from Houhai Lake stands out from the others in being a converted Daoist temple. As good a place as any to meditate over a beer as you contemplate the religious statuary.

🔼 G2 ✉ 37 Yandai Xiejie, Xicheng District ☎ 6404 2778 ◉ Daily 5pm–late
🚌 5, 58, 204

## J J DISCO

This large and ultra-cool nightclub, close to the fashionably down-at-heel Zhengjue Hutong, is popular with locals and visitors alike for its nightly shindigs and for the special party events hosted by Western DJs.

🔼 G2 ✉ 74–76 Xinjiekou Beidajie, Xicheng District

---

### BEIJING INTERNET

The Beijing cyber scene has never been the same since the evening in June 2002 when four local teenagers set fire to an internet café in the Haidian District, causing the deaths of 24 people. The government's response was to close down more than 2,400 unlicensed premises, few of which were ever allowed to reopen. Today's cyber cafés are carefully regulated and few in number. At On/Off bar and restaurant, you can surf the net to your heart's content while listening to good music (🔼 M3 ✉ 5 Xingfu Yicun Xili, off Xingfucunzhong Lu, Chaoyang District ☎ 6415 8083 ◉ 7pm–2am).

---

☎ 6618 9305 ◉ Daily 8pm–2am 🚌 22, 105, 107

## PRINCE GONG'S THEATER

See performances of Beijing opera in a beautifully decorated 19th-century private theater. Times vary, but if you sign up for the guided tour of the residence (▷ 83) between 8.30am and 4.30pm, it's part of the deal.

🔼 F2 ✉ 17 Qianhai Xijie, Xicheng District ☎ 6616 8149
◉ Daily 8.30am–4.30pm
🚌 107, 111, 118

## SAN WEI BOOKSTORE

The floor above the book-selling area is a teahouse by day and a buzzing bar at night. The unusual decor suits the music, usually either live classical Chinese fare or laid-back jazz. Well worth a visit for the cultural experience.

🔼 D6 ✉ 60 Fuxingmennei Dajie, Xicheng District (opposite Minzu Hotel) ☎ 6601 3204 ◉ Daily 9.30am–10.30pm 🚇 Fuxingmen

## WHAT? BAR

Pop fans squeeze into this tiny bar space to watch the local rock bands perform. Listen in while enjoying what must be some of the cheapest drinks in the city.

🔼 G5 ✉ 72 Beichang Jie, Xicheng District ◉ Daily 2pm–late 🚌 5

# Restaurants

Prices are approximate, based on a 3-course meal for one person.
YYY    over 250 yuan
YY     100–250 yuan
Y      under 100 yuan

## CAFÉ SAMBAL (YY–YYY)
Named after the fiery relish that spices up many of its dishes, this chic eatery near the Bell Tower occupies a refurbished *hutong* courtyard house replete with antique furnishings, which adds a romantic air to dining on delicate curries, seafood and other Malaysian specialties.
🛑 G1 ✉ 43 Doufouchi Hutong, Xicheng District ☎ 8403 2131 🕓 Daily 12–12 🚇 Guloudajie 🚌 5, 58, 204, 306

## FANGSHAN (YYY)
Court recipes once reserved for emperors' meals in the 19th century form the basis of the elaborate imperial cuisine served at this renowned restaurant in Beihai Park. Sumptuous imperial-style surroundings.
🛑 F4 ✉ 1 Wenjin Jie (inside the east gate of Beihai Park) ☎ 6401 1879/1889 🕓 Daily 11am–1.30pm, 5–8 🚌 5, 13, 101, 102, 103, 107, 109, 111

## FOOD ST. (Y–YY)
Behind the Xiyuan Hotel, close to the zoo, this is an excellent place to try northern Chinese cuisine at affordable prices. There are varied fresh fish dishes, noodles with shredded chicken, sweet dumplings and "delicacies" such as deep-fried scorpions. The barbecued meat served on skewers is recommended.
🛑 Off map, west of A2 ✉ 1 Sanlihe Lu, Haidian District ☎ 6831 3388 🕓 Lunch and dinner daily 🚇 Xizhimen

## GOLDEN PALACE (YY)
An elegant place to enjoy Chinese cuisine in clean and comfortable surroundings. The menu is divided into sections from regions around China— why not try something from each category? The noodle soup with double-boiled spare ribs is worth trying, as are the sautéed wild vegetables with shredded pork.
🛑 Off map, west of A2

✉ New Century Hotel, Shoudu Tiyuguannan, Haidian District ☎ 6849 2001 🕓 Lunch and dinner daily 🚇 Xizhimen

## HUTONG PIZZA (Y)
Though probably not an ideal alternative to Pizza Hut for the kids, this plain but friendly backstreet pizzeria is fine for a quick lunch or snack for anyone exploring the Back Lakes area and who doesn't want to linger over a Chinese meal.
🛑 G2 ✉ 9 Yingdingqiao Hutong, Xicheng District ☎ 6617 5916 🕓 Daily 11–11 🚌 107, 111, 118

## KAOROU JI (YY)
This Muslim restaurant on the shore of Qianhai Lake has been around for more than a century. The menu (in English with pictures of some dishes) includes fried duck shashlik (kabob), stewed camel in pear and roast duck complete with head. The staff speak little English but are friendly and helpful. In summer there are tables on the balcony but these need to be reserved in advance. The restaurant has its own dinner-boat that sails on the lake.
🛑 G2 ✉ 14 Qianhai Dongyan, Xicheng District ☎ 6404 2554 🕓 Lunch and dinner daily 🚌 58, 204, 306

## LI JIA CAI IMPERIAL RESTAURANT (YYY)
The founder of this tiny

and highly regarded restaurant was the great granddaughter of an employee in the Qing court, who obtained the menus for Empress Dowager Cixi's meals. The restaurant, part of a family home, serves imperial dishes accompanied by a number of Li family and Beijing dishes.

✚ F2 ✉ 11 Yangfang Hutong, Deshengmennei Dajie, Xicheng District ☎ 6618 0107 ⏰ Daily 4–10pm (reservations up to 2 weeks in advance are necessary) 🚇 Jishuitan

### MEI FU (YYY)

This elegant restaurant in a *hutong* near Prince Gong's Residence is dedicated to the memory of the legendary Beijing opera star, Mei Lanfang. Guests are treated to muted recordings of his performances while dining from one of several set menus, including the singer's favorite dishes. The setting is a beautifully restored courtyard house.

✚ F2 ✉ 24 Daxiangfeng Hutong, Xicheng District ☎ 6612 6847 ⏰ Lunch and dinner daily 🚌 95

### MOSCOW (Y–YY)

The reason to come here is to dine surrounded by faded elegance, under chandeliers and amid fluted columns. While the spicy borscht is still worth ordering, some dishes can be disappointing. Try steak with mushroom sauce or the chicken curry drumsticks.

✚ C3 ✉ 135 Xizhimenwai Dajie, Xicheng District (access by a small road on the west side of the Beijing Exhibition Center; look for Mockba Pectopan a short walk down on the right) ☎ 6835 4454 ⏰ Daily 11–2, 5–9 🚇 Xizhimen

### NENG REN JU (YY)

If you're looking for Sichuan hot pot with a twist, check out the boiled lamb dish, which is cooked in a soup of vegetables and spices and then served on a separate plate so you can dip the lamb in a peanut sauce flavored with chili and cilantro (coriander).

✚ D4 ✉ 5 Taipingqiao Dajie, Baitasi, Xicheng District ☎ 6601 2560 ⏰ Daily 10am–2am 🚇 Fuchengmen 🚌 7, 38

### NUAGE (YY–YYY)

This graceful Vietnamese restaurant occupies a handsome lakefront villa that mixes traditional Chinese and Indochinese design motifs. Patio tables afford fine views of Houhai Lake and other sights. The sautéed tamarind crab is among the house specialties.

✚ G2 ✉ 22 Qianhai Dongyan, Xicheng District ☎ 6401 9581 ⏰ Daily 11–10 (10.30 Fri–Sat) 🚌 58, 204, 306

### SICHUAN RESTAURANT (YY)

Overlooks the lobby of the Xiyuan Hotel. Be sure to try the Eight Treasures tea or the hotel's own strong brew of Kaiser beer. Spiced chicken is a fine cold appetizer and braised fish in black-bean sauce a typical main course. The fried walnuts make a delicious dessert.

✚ Off map, west of A2 ✉ Xiyuan Hotel, 1 Sanlihe Lu, Haidian District ☎ 6831 3388 ⏰ Lunch and dinner daily 11–2, 6.30–10.30 🚇 Xizhimen

### YUEMING LOU (Y)

A former church gets a tasteful makeover and becomes a temple to *lao beijing cai* (traditional Beijing cooking) with its uncompromising use of seasonings and rich sauces. Signature dishes include *congbao yangrou* (lamb fried with scallions/ spring onions) and *su hezi* (vegetable dumplings).

✚ F2 ✉ 21A Ya'er Hutong, Xicheng District ☎ 6400 2069 ⏰ Daily 10am–11pm 🚇 Guloudajie

---

### EIGHT TREASURES TEA

A specialty of Sichuan restaurants is Eight Treasures tea, served from the longest teapot you are ever likely to see. The eight ingredients are: jasmine, jujule, walnut, fruit of Chinese wolfberry, raisin, crystal sherry, ginseng and dried longan pulp. The taste is slightly spicy, and prepares you for the spicy flavors to come.

Beijing stands at the center of a constellation of stellar attractions, ranging from the Great Wall of China, through monumental imperial tombs and palaces, to places of outstanding natural beauty.

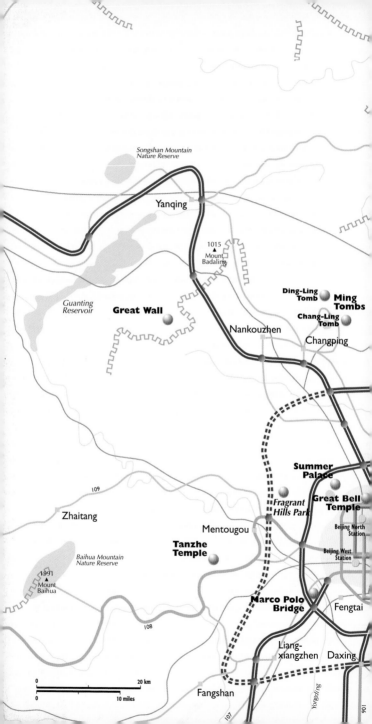

Songshan Mountain
Nature Reserve

Yanqing

1015
▲ Mount
Badaling

Ding-Ling
Tomb **Ming Tombs**

Guanting
Reservoir

**Great Wall**

Chang-Ling
Tomb

Nankouzhen

Changping

109

Zhaitang

**Summer Palace**

*Fragrant
Hills Park*

**Great Bell Temple**

Beijing North
Station

Mentougou

Beijing West
Station

**Tanzhe
Temple**

Baihua Mountain
Nature Reserve

1991
▲ Mount
Baihua

**Marco Polo
Bridge**

Fengtai

Liang-
xiangzhen Daxing

108

0                    20 km

0            10 miles

Fangshan

107

*Yongding*

901

# Fragrant Hills Park

*Gateway at Zhao Miao (left); view of the lake (middle); bronze Milefo statue (right)*

## THE BASICS

🔲 Off map to northwest

✉ 12 miles (20km) west of Beijing

☎ 6259 1155

🕐 6am–7pm (6.30pm in winter)

🚌 333 from the Summer Palace; 360 from the zoo

♿ Inexpensive; cable car moderate; Azure Clouds Temple extra

## HIGHLIGHTS

● Incense-Burner Peak
● Azure Clouds Temple
● Temple of Brilliance
● Autumn colors

## TIP

● Considering the time it takes to get out here, the terrain and the extensive area covered by the park, it makes sense to do this as a full-day outing.

**Popular with Beijingers as well as with tourists, this erstwhile royal hunting territory offers fresh air, bracing walks and superb views of the countryside from the top of the highest peak, Incense-Burner Peak, reached by cable car or on foot. In fall the slopes are a blaze of red.**

**Country park** Fragrant Hills was landscaped with pavilions, lakes and teahouses during the reign of Emperor Qianlong. The 395-acre (160ha) park was opened to the public in 1956 and proved an immediate hit.

**Temples** Just inside the northern gate is Azure Clouds Temple, a must-see for its stunning architecture. Built as a nunnery in 1331, most of the halls date from the Ming dynasty. Two fierce deities, Heng (Dragon) and Ha (Tiger), stand guard outside Mountain Gate Hall, warding off evil spirits. The temple is famous for its stupas (tiered towers), but also has carp ponds, fountains and 500-year-old cypresses. China's first president, Sun Yat Sen, was interred in the Vayra Throne Pagoda while a permanent mausoleum in Nanjing was under construction. The Temple of Brilliance (Zhao Miao) is a large Tibetan style lamasery complex built in 1780 as the residence for the sixth Panchen Lama during his visits to Emperor Qianlong. Surviving treasures are a majestic glazed-tiled archway in front of the complex, a Tibetan-style terrace and a glazed-tile pagoda.

*The Great Bell Temple is home to what was once the largest bell in China*

# Great Bell Temple

**This unique little museum is in a Buddhist temple where you will see the Yongle Bell, the second largest bell in China. A visit here is a rewarding experience and the music of the temple's Bell Orchestra is a surprising pleasure.**

**Tons of bells** The temple-museum is home to hundreds of bronze bells from all over China, but pride of place rests with a 46.5-ton giant bell cast in the Ming dynasty and known as the Yongle Bell. It hangs on a huge wooden frame by a 3ft-long (1m) iron and steel nail coated with copper. The nail is 2in (6cm) wide and pierces two U-shape hooks around the wooden block. It is calculated that each 3/100sq in (0.2sq cm) of the nail can withstand 5.25lb (2.4kg) of shearing stress. For centuries, the bell was the greatest in China, until it was edged out by a 50-ton bell cast to celebrate the millennium. Displays in the temple-museum (in English) explain the technology of bell-casting in China.

**Ring the bells** You can get into the spirit of bell-ringing by thumping a large one outside the temple with the help of a small battering ram. Inside the temple, for a nominal fee, you can dip your hand into a large bowl of water before ferociously rubbing its twin handles to produce a musical vibration. If a certain frequency is attained, the vibrations cause spurts of water to appear–thus the bowl's nickname, "Dragon Fountain." A narrow staircase leads to a platform above the giant Yongle Bell, where there is a history of the bell.

## THE BASICS

➕ Off map to northwest
✉ 31A Beisanhuan Xilu (Third Ring Road), Haidian District
☎ 6255 0819
🕐 Daily 8.30–4.30
🚇 Xizhimen
🚌 302, 367
♿ None
💰 Inexpensive

## HIGHLIGHTS

● Yongle Bell
● Bell-ringing practice
● The temple itself

## TIP

● The music of the Giant Bell Orchestra may be purchased on CD or cassette. If you decide to buy one, play it first to make sure that your copy works.

# The Great Wall

*The Great Wall's bricks could encircle the earth in a 16ft-high (5m) wall*

## THE BASICS

➕ Off map to north

✉ Badaling in Yanqing County; Mutianyu in Huairou County; Simatai in Miyun County

☎ Badaling 6912 2222; Mutianyu 6964 2022; Simatai 6903 1051

🕐 Badaling daily 7am–5.30pm; Mutianyu 7.30am–6pm; Simatai 8–5

🍴 Restaurants and teashops at Badaling and Mutianyu

🚌 Tourist buses 1, 2, 3 from Qianmen terminal for Badaling; minibuses from Dongzhimen bus station for Mutianyu. No convenient bus access to Simatai

🚇 Qinglongqiao

♿ None

💰 Moderate to expensive

❓ Hotels organize tours but consider simply taking a taxi from Beijing for a day

## HIGHLIGHTS

● Badaling: easily accessible but touristy
● Simatai: less busy but also less restored
● Mutianyu: set in a scenic area

**Former President Nixon exclaimed to his Secretary of State, "I think you would have to agree, Mr. Secretary, that this is a great wall." A visit on a snowy winter day can be so quiet it feels like "your wall."**

**Significance** Mao Zedong said that anyone wishing to be a hero must first climb the wall, and for many Chinese people, the wall remains very much a part of their cultural identity. It was built between the 5th century BC and the 16th century AD; its purpose was protective, although it served also as a military communications route. The building of the wall was often associated with acts of great cruelty. Emperors like Qin Shi Huang in the 3rd century BC became infamous for their mobilization of enforced labor. From the 17th century onward it was left to crumble away, a process that was accelerated by neighboring peasants seeking building material.

**Avoiding the crowds** Ask a few questions before settling for one of the many available tours. Which part of the wall does the tour visit? Badaling, restored in the 1950s, is the most popular location but, be warned, is crowded and commercialized; a cable car helps the large number of visitors. Simatai requires some fitness and fortitude, as sections of the unrestored wall are unprotected at the sides. Mutianyu is accessible and safe and, like Badaling, offers a cable-car ride so it can be overcrowded. Check how much time is spent at the wall; beware of time-consuming and often unrewarding trips to factory stores along the way.

# Ming Tombs

● The mythological *xiechi*, a cat-like creature with horns, one of the six pairs of animals lining the Spirit Way

● The original, unpainted pillars supporting the Palace of Sacrificing, made from entire trunks of the nanmu tree

● Jewelry on show in the Palace of Sacrificing

● The royal treasures from Ding Ling

## TIP

● Only the Ding Ling tomb has been fully excavated. You may find that it is enough to visit this one and to stroll the Spirit Way to get an adequate picture of the site.

**Willows whisper in the wind as the stone figures along the Spirit Way stare imperiously at visitors following in the steps of mourners who carried Ming emperors to their resting place.**

**Death of an emperor** Of the 17 emperors who ruled during the Ming dynasty (1368–1644), 13 were ceremoniously laid to rest in this beautiful place about 30 miles (48km) northwest of their capital. The site was chosen for its geomantic qualities—facing Beijing, with mountains on three sides. Elaborate rites dictated the stages of the funeral. The deceased's concubines were buried alive to comfort the emperor in the next world.

**Not to miss** The ceremonial avenue leading to the tombs, the Spirit Way, provides a wonderful

*Chang Ling, the tomb of Emperor Yongle (left); rows of flowers outside the gateway to the Ming Tombs (right)*

opportunity to admire 18th-century Ming sculptures in their original context. Only three of the tombs are open to the public. At the end of the avenue one of them, Chang Ling, comes into view. Emperor Yongle was interred here in 1424, and the focus of interest at this tomb is the imposing Palace of Sacrificing and its collection of imperial riches. A model of the whole site is on show and the exhibits carry descriptions in English. At the rear of the palace, there is a stele tower, a column with inscriptions, while an undis-tinguished mound behind railings at the back marks the actual burial ground. Of the other two tombs, only the excavated Ding Ling is worth a visit. A staircase leads to the burial vault holding a replica of the excavated coffin. In the courtyard, relics of the emperor and his two empresses are on display.

## THE BASICS

+ Off map to north
✉ Shisanling, Changping County
☎ 6976 1424
🕐 Daily 8–5.30
🍴 Most tours include lunch at the Friendship Store
🚌 Tourist buses 1, 2, 3, 4, 5
♿ None
💰 Moderate to expensive

# Summer Palace

**HIGHLIGHTS**

● Kunming Lake
● Marble Boat
● Bridge with Seventeen Arches
● Hall of Benevolence and Longevity

**TIP**

● Buying the Gate Ticket can be a false economy as it excludes admission to the Garden of Virtue and Harmony and the Tower of Buddhist Incense, two sights well worth seeing.

**The largest imperial garden in China, strewn with palaces and architectural flights of fancy, is arguably Beijing's most precious gem.**

**The ultimate playground** Members of Beijing's imperial court selected an area northwest of the city for a summer resort. What you see today was laid out in the 18th century, but toward the end of the following century Empress Dowager Cixi misappropriated funds intended for the navy and spent it instead on a lavish rebuilding program for her Summer Palace. Mindful, perhaps, of her debt to the navy, she commissioned the white Marble Boat (a wooden paddleboat structure on a marble base) that is berthed at the edge of the lake. The Summer Palace was ransacked and torched in 1900 at the hands of Anglo-French troops intent

*Visitors on Longevity Hill (far left); a pavilion on the lake in the Garden of Harmonious Pleasure (middle); musicians perform in the theater (right); a pavilion on Kunming Lake (bottom left); rowing under the Seventeen Arch Bridge on Kunming Lake (bottom middle); painting in the Long Corridor (bottom right)*

on revenge after the Boxer Rebellion, but rebuilding began soon after. A major restoration was completed in the 1950s.

**Walking guide** Enter the grounds through the East Gate and note first the Hall of Benevolence and Longevity, where Cixi conducted official business. Stretched out behind the hall is the expanse of Kunming Lake, used for ice-skating in winter. Keep it on your left, passing the Hall of Jade Ripples before entering the painted Long Corridor. Near the end of this walkway are a coffee shop, the Marble Boat and a jetty where boat rides and rowboats (or, in winter, skates) are available for trips to the Seventeen Arch Bridge, which stretches from the shore to South Lake Island. Plan to spend at least three hours here enjoying the attractions.

**THE BASICS**

✚ Off map to northwest
✉ Yíheyuanlu, Haidian District
☎ 6288 1144
🕐 Daily 7–7
🍴 Coffee shop and restaurant
🚇 Xízhimen, then bus 375
🚌 301, 303, 332, 333, 346, 384, 726, 904
👆 Moderate

# Old Summer Palace

*Despite the broken masonry (right), the palace retains traces of its former splendor (middle and left)*

## THE BASICS

➕ Off map to northwest
✉ Qinghua Xilu 28, Haidian District; just over 1 mile (2km) east of the Summer Palace
☎ 6262 8501
🕐 Daily 7–7
Ⓧ Xizhimen
🚍 375 minibus from Xizhimen subway station
🎫 Park: inexpensive; ruins: moderate

### HIGHLIGHTS

● Museum with models and drawings giving some idea of the pre-1860 splendor
● Restored concrete maze

### TIP

● The Old Summer Palace is within walking distance (or a short taxi ride) of the New Summer Palace (▷ 100–101), which opens up the possibility of escaping from the crowds that habitually infest the latter.

**The grounds and ruins of the original Summer Palace are enchanting. Stand quietly and you can imagine fabulously clothed emperors and empresses, attended by scores of servants, at play.**

**East meets West** Remnants of baroque pillars and ruins of grand fountains are a tantalizing hint of the artistic exuberance and sheer splendor that once characterized this royal playground. First laid out in the 12th century, it became the emperor's summer retreat from the 15th century until 1860. Artistic styling took flight under Emperor Qianlong in the second half of the 18th century and, though ostensibly created as an act of devotion to his mother, the project took on the feel of an architectural binge. The emperor journeyed south, accompanied by artists to make sketches, to fulfill a desire to reproduce in the north the garden landscapes of southern China. The Jesuit architects, Sichelbarth and Benoist, designed Western-style buildings, including gazebos and follies, in a blending of West and East. The results were the Garden of Perfect Brightness, the Garden of Eternal Spring and the Garden of Beautiful Spring.

**Elgin masonry** The broken masonry of the Old Summer Palace bears testimony to the destructive visit of British and French troops during the Second Opium War. In 1860, Lord Elgin ordered the site to be burned after his soldiers had thoroughly looted it—some of their plunder can be seen in London's British Museum and the Louvre in Paris.

# More to See

## CHINA PUPPET THEATER

Shadow and hand puppets are used expertly here to tell traditional folk tales, which appeal to adults and children alike. This is a fading art, so an opportunity to see a show is well worth taking. Many cover traditional Chinese themes, but there are also Western fairy tales and stories.

➕ Off map to north ✉ 1A, Anhua Xilu, off Beisanhuan Lu (Third Ring Road), Chaoyang District ☎ 6425 4798 🕐 Sat 10.30am, 3pm; Sun 3pm 💷 Moderate 🚌 300, 302, 367, 387

## MARCO POLO BRIDGE

One reason scholars question whether Marco Polo ever made it to China is that he never mentioned the Great Wall. The Western name of the bridge alludes to his putative 1290 visit and his detailed description of the structure. Spanning the River Yongding, it was built in 1192 and restored in the 17th century, and is noted for an 18th-century stele with a calligraphic inscription by Emperor Qianlong. On each side of the bridge are parapets with hundreds of carved lions surmounting the columns. In 1937 the bridge was the site of the opening shots in the war against Japanese invaders. The Memorial Hall of the War of Resistance against Japan (Kangri Zhanzheng Jinianguan), on the Beijing side, marks this event.

➕ Off map to southwest ✉ Wanping City, Fengtai District ☎ Bridge: 8389 3919; museum: 8389 2355 🕐 Daily 6am–9pm; museum: 8.30–6 🚌 339 💷 Inexpensive

## TANZHE TEMPLE

This Buddhist temple to the west of Beijing is the largest in the area. It dates back to the 3rd century AD and contains decorative features not found elsewhere in Beijing. The temple was originally patronized by Princess Miaoyan, a daughter of Kublai Khan. It is noted for its scenic setting in a hilly region, its trees of various species, and a pond called the Dragon Pool.

➕ Off map to west ✉ Tanzhesi, Mentougou ☎ 6086 2505 🕐 Jun–Oct daily 8–5.30; Nov–May daily 8–4.30 🚌 7, 336, 931 💷 Inexpensive

*Marco Polo Bridge*

# Excursions

## EASTERN QING TOMBS

**A drive through scenic countryside brings you to the spectacularly situated tombs of some of the Qing dynasty rulers, their wives and concubines.**

The extensive valley site is, if anything, more interesting than the better-advertised and far busier, but older, Ming tombs (▷ 98–99). Five emperors are buried here, including Shunzhi (1643–61), the first Qing (Manchu) ruler. Each of their grandiose tombs is approached along a Spirit Way. The notorious Empress Dowager Cixi had her tomb rebuilt after the death of her husband Ci'an, making it one of the most elaborate of the imperial tombs. The easiest ways to get here from the capital are on an organized tour or by taxi.

### THE BASICS

www.qingdongling.com
**Distance:** 80 miles (128km) northeast of Beijing
**Journey Time:** Around 3 hours by bus
✉ Near Malanyu, Zunhua County
☎ 0315 694 5475
🕐 Jun–Sep daily 8.30–5.30; Oct–May daily 9–4.30
🚌 Qing Dong Ling bus
💰 Expensive

## WESTERN QING TOMBS

**For the location of his mausoleum, Emperor Yongzheng (1723–35) selected this new site a long way from the Eastern Qing Tombs, where his perhaps not-so-esteemed ancestors were interred.**

With the sequence of imperial burials broken, the Qing rulers now had a choice when it came to their final resting place, and a further three emperors, four empresses and assorted minions decided to settle here. The site, which is rich in traditional Chinese architecture and sculpture, occupies a scenic setting in the forested foothills of the Yongning Mountains. Yongzheng's Tai Ling Tomb, reached via a Spirit Way, is just one of the tombs and tumuli that can be visited. The necropolis's most recent imperial resident is Puyi, China's last emperor, whose ashes are buried in an ordinary cemetery rather than in a monumental tomb.

### THE BASICS

**Distance:** 87 miles (140km) southwest of Beijing
**Journey Time:** Around 3.5 hours by bus
✉ Outside Yixian town, Yixian County
☎ 0312 694 5471
🕐 Daily 8.30–5.30
🚌 Yixian bus
💰 Expensive

## THE BASICS

**Distance:** 112 miles
(180km) northeast of
Beijing
**Journey Time:** Around
4 hours by bus
✉ Outside Santunying
town, Qianxi County
☎ 0315 584 4024
🕐 Daily 8.30–5.30
🚌 Santunying bus
✋ Inexpensive

## JINGZHONG MOUNTAIN

**This holy mountain, which reaches an
elevation of 2,001ft (610m), draws
pilgrims upward to its constellation of
Ming dynasty Buddhist, Confucian and
Daoist temples and other shrines, which
were further enhanced during the following Qing dynasty.**

Due in part to its popularity as a religious site
(traces of this use date back to the Song dynasty),
and a scenic, craggy and pine-forested setting, the
mountain is being developed as a tourist area,
with forest walks, adventure play areas, health
resorts, a cable car and other facilities already in
place, and more being planned. Pilgrims can reach
many of the temples by climbing the 1,871 steps
of the Sacred Way. The easiest way to visit the
mountain from Beijing is on an organized tour,
with final access from traditional villages at its
base, among them Liaozhuang, Mengzhuang,
Nanyangzhuang and Zhishanzhuang.

## THE BASICS

**Distance:** 37 miles (60km)
southwest of Beijing
**Journey Time:** Around
2 hours by bus
✉ Zhoukoudian, Fangshan
District ☎ 6930 1272
🕐 8.30–4.30
🚌 From Haihutun bus
station in Beijing (get off at
Zhoukoudian)
🚆 From Yongdingmen rail
station in Beijing
✋ Inexpensive

## ZHOUKOUDIAN (PEKING MAN SITE)

**In 1921, excavations near the village
of Zhoukoudian revealed evidence of
Paleolithic man—*Homo erectus
Pekinensis*—dating back more than
500,000 years. Bones of more than
40 individuals were identified.**

You can wander around the site and, in the
adjacent museum, see replicas of anthropological
finds and remains of extinct creatures that must
have terrified Peking Man. The skull of Peking Man
disappeared during World War II, when it was
taken out of the country for safekeeping and it has
never been found.

Beijing caters to all, having a good selection of budget, mid-range and luxury hotels. With many of the first two categories aimed at Chinese travelers, rates are generally lower than might be expected.

# Introduction

The standard of hotels is now high in Beijing. The number of top-end hotels is expanding fast, fueled by China's booming economy, surging inbound tourism and the 2008 Olympics. More affordable mid-range and budget hotels are also opening. The Beijing Municipal Tourism Bureau is aiming for more than 800 star-rated hotels with 130,000 rooms by the Olympics—double the number in 2000.

## Range of Accommodations

A central location is somewhat less important in Beijing than in other major cities, as many of the principal sights are outside the city. Beijing is a vast, sprawling place that's far from easy to get around quickly or comfortably, so you might want to opt for a more expensive hotel in an area that's close to where you want to be. Several hotels are within walking distance of Tian'anmen Square and there is a cluster of luxury hotels in Beijing's northeast corner. Beijing also has a number of less expensive hotels built in the 1950s, before the open door policy, such as the sprawling Friendship Hotel, originally constructed for Russian experts brought in to help rebuild the city. At the less expensive end of the market there are hotels and hostels with triples or dormitory-style rooms. They are inexpensive but the barrack-like rooms, although likely to be clean, provide no privacy.

### STARS IN THEIR COURSES

The hotel star rating system employed in China can often be a reliable guide to what you can expect from a hotel, but not always, and may even be misleading in some cases. The nationally determined five-star category generally means what it says, though many hotels that are a decade or two old have seen no modernization or upgrading, or even a lick of paint, since they were built. Four- and three-star hotels might have been "assisted" to their status by a "sympathetic" local official. Two- and one-star hotels can be surprisingly dowdy and may even have safety issues. Renovations and upgrading do occur, but the picture is patchy.

# Budget Hotels

## BEIJING GOLDEN PALACE SILVER STREET HOTEL

Modern 3-star hotel only a few minutes' walk from the shopping malls and boutiques of Wangfujing Dajie and Sun Dong An Market. All 108 rooms are comfortable, clean and great value.

🚇 J5 ✉ 31 Ganyu Hutong, Wangfujing Dajie, Dongcheng District ☎ 8511 0388 🚉 Dengshikou

## BEIJING LIEN HOTEL

www.lien.com.cn
Downtown budget hotel with clean rooms, color TV, private baths and all upscale amenities at a fraction of a luxury price.

🚇 L3 ✉ 3 Xinzhong Xi Jie, Goungti Bei Lu (off East 2nd Ring Road) ☎ 6553 1503 🚉 Dongsishitiao

## DONG FANG

www.bjdongfanghotel.com.cn
Value hotel with good facilities. In the Qianmen area, the Dong Fang has eight restaurants, a sauna, gym, business center and a laundry. All 320 rooms are air-conditioned.

🚇 F8 ✉ 11 Wanming Lu, Xuanwu District ☎ 6301 4466 🚉 59, 105

## FANGYUAN

Tucked away down a street off Wangfujing. Its 50 rooms are rather drab but good value because it is so central.

🚇 H5 ✉ 36 Dengshikouxi Jie, Dongcheng District ☎ 6525 6311 🚉 Dengshikou 🚉 103, 104, 111

## FAR EAST YOUTH HOSTEL

Affordable rooms (78) in the heart of the Dazhalan area, within walking distance of Tian'anmen Square. There is a Chinese restaurant.

🚇 F8 ✉ 90 Tieshuxie Jie, Xuanwu District ☎ 6301 8811 🚉 Qianmen

## GUOZHAN

This modern hotel is an affordable option for anyone seeking budget accommodations within reach of good food—the Royal Café of the Radisson SAS hotel (▷ 112) and a huge supermarket are across the street. The hotel has 70 standard rooms with air-conditioning and a Sichuan restaurant.

🚇 Off map, north of M1 ✉ 10 Jiagan Xi Lu, Chaoyang District ☎ 6463 9922 🚉 302, 379

## LU SONG YUAN

www.the-silk-road.com
This is a charming, traditional choice, close to Tian'anmen Square. It is styled like the surrounding historic buildings with multiple courtyards and pagoda-style roofs. Despite appearances, it has an up-to-date business center and internet access.

🚇 H2 ✉ 22 Banchang Hutong, Kuanjie ☎ 6404 0436 🚉 Zhangzizhonglu

## RAINBOW

www.rainbowhotel.com.cn
A decent modern, 300-room Chinese hotel, with few foreign visitors and little English spoken, in the interesting Qianmen area.

🚇 F9 ✉ 11 Xijing Lu, Xuanwu District ☎ 6301 2266 🚉 59, 106, 343

## TIANRUI

An attractive budget option in downtown, near Wangfujing shopping street and the night market. The modern rooms are tastefully decorated, and there's a gym, sauna, indoor swimming pool and babysitting service.

🚇 J5 ✉ 15 Baishu Hutong, Dongcheng District ☎ 6526 6699 🚉 Dengshikou

**WHERE TO STAY  BUDGET HOTELS**

# Mid-Range Hotels

## BAMBOO GARDEN HOTEL
www.bbgh.com.cn
In a quiet lane near the Drum Tower, yet only a five-minute walk from the subway. Each of the 40 rooms is equipped with satellite TV but if you are to enjoy your stay you must have a balcony overlooking the garden.

✚ F1 ✉ 24 Xiaoshiqiao Hutong (off Jiugulou Dajie), Xicheng District ☎ 5852 0088 Ⓜ Guloudajie

## BEIJING DONGJIAOMINXIANG HOTEL
www.bjdjmx.com
What most recommends this hotel is its superb location in the leafy former legation quarter about seven minutes' walk from Tian'anmen Square. Though it caters mainly to Chinese businessmen, the reception staff speak English and are generally helpful. The rooms are comfortable, if a little small.

✚ H6 ✉ 23 Dongjiaominxiang, Dongcheng District ☎ 6524 3311 Ⓜ Qianmen

## COMFORT INN & SUITES
www.choicehotels.com
This hotel, in a streamlined modern tower

block, is convenient for Sanlitun bar street and local restaurants like Serve the People (▷ 76). Geared to leisure as well as business travelers, the rooms are clean and comfortable. There's a small swimming pool on the roof and bicycle rental is available. A Continental breakfast is included.

✚ Off map, east of M3 ✉ 6 Gongti Beilu, Chaoyang District ☎ 8523 5522 🚌 113

## HAOYUAN
www.haoyuanhotel.com
Having only 18 rooms, this *hutong* hotel in a tiled-roof, Qing-era building attracts visitors who want something more Chinese than is on offer in an anonymous tower hotel. Reserve as far ahead as possible. Antique and antique-style furniture and vases grace

the public spaces and guest rooms, ranged around two garden courtyards. Nearby restaurants in the down-at-heel *hutong* serve Beijing fare.

✚ J5 ✉ 53 Shijia Hutong, Dongsinan Dajie, Dongcheng District ☎ 6512 5557 Ⓜ Dengshikou 🚌 11, 103, 106

## HOLIDAY INN DOWNTOWN BEIJING
www.ichotelsgroup.com
Conveniently close to a subway station and shopping malls. It has a good recreation center, an affordable Western-style restaurant and 347 rooms.

✚ C3 ✉ 98 Beilishi Lu, Xicheng District ☎ 6833 8822 Ⓜ Chegongzhuang

## HOLIDAY INN LIDO BEIJING
www.beijing-lido.holiday-inn.com
Though a bit remote from the sights, this hotel is worth considering for its first-rate amenities. They include a bowling alley and tennis courts, as well as restaurants, a supermarket, pharmacy and indoor swimming pool.

✚ Off map, northeast of M1 ✉ Lido Place, 6 Jiang Tai Lu, Chaoyang District ☎ 6437 6688 🚌 Hotel shuttle bus from Wanfujing

## JIANGUO HOTEL QIANMEN
www.qianmenhotel.com
The refurbished Qianmen, near the Temple of Heaven and Liulichang

Antiques Street, has 400 rooms. The rooms are spacious and airy and there's a sauna and beauty center, a chic lobby, good restaurants, a gym, and billiard room. Rates are at the lower end of the price category.
🔲 F8 ✉ 175 Yong'an Lu, Xuanwu District ☎ 6301 6688 🚍 15, 23, 25, 102

## MINZU
www.minzuhotel.cn
A good hotel in a useful location just west of the city center. The 607 rooms are pleasantly decorated. Facilities include a gym and a billiards room.
🔲 D6 ✉ 51 Fuxingmennei Dajie, Xicheng District ☎ 6601 4466 🚇 Xidan

## NOVOTEL PEACE
www.novotel.com
This hotel, at the top end of the price range, is in the heart of the city, with 337 rooms, indoor pool and restaurants.
🔲 J5 ✉ 3 Jinyu Hutong, Dongcheng District ☎ 6512 8833 🚇 Dengshikou 🚍 104, 111

## OCEAN
www.cosco.com.hk
In an up-and-coming commercial area whose nightclubs come alive with neon at night, this smart, modern, 84-room hotel is within walking distance of the Forbidden City.
🔲 J6 ✉ 189 Dongsinan Jie, Dongcheng District ☎ 6523 2574 🚍 110, 116

## RED CAPITAL RESIDENCE
www.redcapitalclub.com.cn
"Mao chic" is how Red Capital's American owner has described the quirky interiors of this boutique hotel. Antique carved wooden beds, furniture from the offices of former party officials, birdcages and goldfish bowls are used to decorate the 200-year-old courtyard house. Under the trapdoor in the courtyard is a wine bar showing films from the Cultural Revolution. The hotel is unmarked: Look for the red door with the number 9.
🔲 J3 ✉ 9 Dongsi Liutiao, Dongcheng District ☎ 6402 7150 🚇 Zhongzizhonglu 🚍 24

## TIANLUN SONGHE
www.tianlunsonghehotel.com
The Songhe is well

### HOTEL SERVICE
Many hotels now provide access to the internet for their guests, for a fee. They generally have computers—everything from a single computer in the lobby to a full-fledged business center. Paid-for connections for guests' own laptops range from simple dial-up connections using the room phone line, to broadband Ethernet connections and Wi-Fi hot spots in the lobby or throughout the hotel.

versed in the art of dealing with Western visitors and conveniently close to Wangfujing Dajie and the Forbidden City. The 310 rooms are at the top end of the category.
🔲 H4 ✉ 88 Dengshikou Dajie, Dongcheng District ☎ 6513 8822 🚇 Dengshikou 🚍 111, 108

## YOUHAO GUESTHOUSE
A character-rich, 30-room *hutong* lodging a few blocks east of the Drum Tower, the Youhao lives up to its name—which means Friendship—thanks to a staff who take care of their guests. The villa residence has a handsome courtyard and garden, spare Oriental furnishings and a decent Japanese restaurant. China's pre-Communist leader, Nationalist Generalissimo Chiang Kai Shek, lived here for a time.
🔲 H2 ✉ 7 Houyuan'ensi Hutong, Jiaodaokounan Dajie, Dongcheng District ☎ 6403 1114 🚇 Beixinqiao

## XINDADU
Also called the Beijing Mandarin, this elegant four-star hotel is in the northwest of the city, south of the zoo. It has 530 rooms, a swimming pool, a sauna, fitness center and several restaurants.
🔲 A2 ✉ 21 Chegongzhuangxi Lu, Xicheng District ☎ 6831 9988 🚇 Beijing Zoo (from 2009)

# Luxury Hotels

## BEIJING RAFFLES HOTEL

www.beijing.raffles.com
Beijing's oldest hotel, occupying a prime downtown site on the corner of Wangfujing shopping street and only one metro stop from Tian'anmen Square, was taken over and refurbished by the Raffles chain in 2006. Some of the hotel's original features have been resurrected, including the stunning dance floor with grand piano. There's a fitness suite, squash and tennis courts and a swimming pool.
✚ H6 ✉ 33 Dongchang'an Jie, Dongcheng District ☎ 6526 3388 🚇 Wangfujing

## CHINA WORLD

www.shangri-la.com
Consistently one of Beijing's best hotels, with 738 tastefully furnished rooms, superb restaurants and first-class gym, swimming pool and golf center with two golf simulators.
✚ Off map, east of M6 ✉ 1 Jianguomenwai Dajie, Chaoyang District ☎ 6505 2266 🚇 Guomao 🚌 1, 4, 37, 52

## GREAT WALL SHERATON

www.starwoodhotels.com
In the Sanlitun diplomatic district, a short taxi ride from the city center. This 827-room hotel is built around a seven-story atrium loaded with creature comforts to make your stay ultraluxurious.
✚ Off map, east of M1 ✉ 10 Dongsanhuanbei Lu, Chaoyang District ☎ 6590 5566 🚌 300, 402, 801

## HILTON

www.beijing.hilton.com
Convenient to the airport and the Sanlitun diplomatic and shopping district. Calm and attractive.
✚ Off map, east of M1 ✉ 1, Dongfang Lu, Chaoyang District ☎ 5865 5000 🚌 300, 402, 801

## NIKKO NEW CENTURY

www.newcenturyhotel.com.cn
Good for families and sports-lovers. The recreation center includes a good-size pool, a bowling alley and outdoor tennis courts. 725 rooms.
✚ Off map, west of A2 ✉ 6 Shoudu Tiyuguannan Lu,

Haidian District ☎ 6849 2001 🚇 Baishiqao (from 2009) 🚌 24

## PENINSULA BEIJING

www.peninsula.com
The Peninsula vies with China World as Beijing's best hotel and exudes luxury in 525 rooms. Within walking distance of the Forbidden City. Restaurants, pool, health club and dance club.
✚ J5 ✉ 8 Jinyu Hutong, Dongcheng District ☎ 8516 2888 🚇 Dengshikou 🚌 103, 11, 106

## RADISSON SAS

www.radissonsas.com
Terrific rooms (362), a good-size pool, tennis and squash courts and a Finnish sauna help make the Radisson popular. There is a large supermarket next door.
✚ Off map, north of M1 ✉ 6A Beisanhuandong Lu, Chaoyang District ☎ 5922 3388 🚌 302, 18

## SWISSOTEL

www.swissotel.com
Few hotels in Beijing have geared themselves so successfully and pleasantly to the needs of Western vacationers. A subway station is nearby and the 454 rooms and facilities are generally excellent, including those for visitors with disabilities. Airport shuttle bus.
✚ L4 ✉ Hong Kong Macau Center, 2 Chaoyangmenbei Dajie, Chaoyang District ☎ 6553 2288 🚇 Dongsishitao

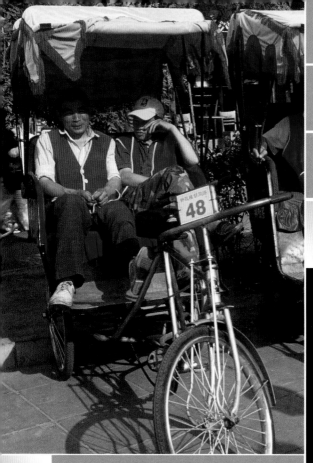

Need to Know

Use this section to help you in planning your visit to Beijing and getting around once you are there. You will also find useful tips and a section on language.

# Planning Ahead

## When to Go

It is best to visit Beijing between September and mid-November, when temperatures are pleasant and there is little rain. Avoid visiting around Chinese New Year (late January or early February) when most places are closed. If you don't mind gray skies and snow flurries, December is worth considering as there are few crowds.

**TIME**

Beijing is 13 hours ahead of New York, 16 hours ahead of Los Angeles and 8 hours ahead of GMT. China does not have daylight saving.

| AVERAGE DAILY MAXIMUM TEMPERATURES | | | | | | | | | | | |
|---|---|---|---|---|---|---|---|---|---|---|---|
| JAN | FEB | MAR | APR | MAY | JUN | JUL | AUG | SEP | OCT | NOV | DEC |
| 25°F | 29°F | 40°F | 57°F | 65°F | 76°F | 81°F | 77°F | 64°F | 57°F | 40°F | 23°F |
| −4°C | −2°C | 5°C | 14°C | 19°C | 24°C | 27°C | 25°C | 18°C | 14°C | 5°C | −5°C |

**Spring** (April to May) is dry, with a wind from the Gobi Desert blowing across the city.

**Summer** (June to August) is uncomfortably hot and very humid.

**Autumn** (September to mid-November) is pleasant, with comfortable temperatures and virtually no rain.

**Winter** (mid-November to March) sees freezing winds from Siberia, which can cause temperatures to plunge to as low as 1°F (−17°C).

## WHAT'S ON

**January** *Spring Festival Concert*.

**January/February** *Chinese New Year* (on the first day of the first moon): The most important festival in the year. Celebrations are held in the Great Bell Temple (▷ 95), Ditan Park and elsewhere.

**February/March** *Lantern Festival*: Also governed by the lunar cycle. Families celebrate together in the evenings, especially in parks. Lanterns are placed on the ground around picnicking groups.

**March/April** *Guanyin's Birthday*: A good time to visit the temples. Guanyin is the goddess of mercy.

**April** *Martial Arts Festival*: Martial arts displays at the Great Wall at Badaling (▷ 96).

*Tomb Sweeping Day/Clear Brightness Festival* (Apr 5; Apr 4 in leap years): Relatives pay respects to their ancestors by sweeping their tombs and burning "ghost money."

**May** *May Day* (1 May): International Labor Day is marked by floral displays citywide and celebrations in Tian'anmen Square.

*Youth Day* (May 4).

**October** *National Day* (Oct 1): The founding of the People's Republic of China is marked by colorful flags, bunting and red lanterns.

*Mid-Autumn Festival* (on the 15th day of the eighth moon): Families picnic, gaze at the moon and eat the traditional moon cakes, filled with lotus root, dates and sesame–an acquired taste.

**October/November** *Beijing Music Festival*: More than 1,000 foreign and home-grown musicians participate in 20 concerts.

## Beijing Online

Suggesting internet sites about China remains a tricky business. The central government continuously monitors websites, and crackdowns are sporadic and unpredictable, unexpectedly blocking sites. At the time of writing, the following sites are available.

### www.beijingpage.com

Everything you need to know about the city, from museums to entertainment, food and drink, and even the weather.

### www.thatsbj.com

Website of the popular English-language listings magazine. Tells you what artists are in town and where to eat, drink and play sports.

### www.btmbeijing.com

The online version of the monthly magazine, *Beijing This Month* is a good, up-to-the-minute source for dining and bar listings.

### www.chinatravelservice.com

The Hong Kong-based travel agency that serves Beijing and offers details of tours, hotels and sightseeing in Beijing and China as a whole.

### http://english.people.com.cn

This is the home page for the Beijing-based English-language *People's Daily*. It's worth visiting for the state spin on news.

### www.scmp.com

The site of the *South China Morning Post*, Hong Kong's English-language daily, used to give more balanced accounts of China's news than any mainland publication. However, in its attempts to gain market share on the mainland, it is becoming less provocative than it was.

### www.tour-beijing.com

This web page of Beijing Xinhua International Tours is a useful source for background information and maps.

| GOOD TRAVEL SITES |
|---|

**www.fodors.com**
A complete travel-planning site. You can research prices and weather; book air tickets, cars and rooms; pose questions (and get answers) to fellow travelers; and find links to other sites.

**www.cits.net**
This official state tourism agency offers details on a range of tour packages, as well as some useful China travel tips.

| INTERNET ACCESS |
|---|

Internet cafés face strict controls and are often shut down. Licenses for new internet cafés are hard to come by. The internet is subjected to censorship and controls in China.
Many hotels now provide access to the internet for their guests, for a fee. Other options are using the computers at public libraries and at Pacific Coffee outlets in the city; and WLAN connections at Starbucks outlets.

# Getting There

Visitors must hold a valid passport, with an expiry date at least six months after arrival, and a visa. A single-entry visa is usually valid for 30 days and must generally be used within three months of issue. Visas usually take three to five working days to obtain and are available through your Chinese Embassy or consulate and through specialist tour operators. One-month visa extensions can sometimes be arranged through the Public Security Bureau ✉ 2 Andingmen Dongdajie ☎ 6404 7799. No vaccinations are required, but some doctors recommend inoculation against Hepatitis A. Always check entry requirements before you travel.

## CUSTOMS

Two liters of any alcohol may be imported. You can bring in up to 400 cigarettes or the same amount of tobacco. You can also import up to 50 grams of gold, and up to 20,000 yuan notes. The importation of foreign currency exceeding US$5,000 should be declared. Chinese currency cannot be exported. Special documentation is required for the export of antiques. Be sure that any antique you have purchased is allowed to be exported; these must bear a red seal.

## AIRPORTS

Beijing Capital Airport is 17 miles (27km) northeast of the city center. This is Beijing's only significant airport and most airlines with flights to China come into Beijing. There are two adjoining terminals for international and domestic flights.

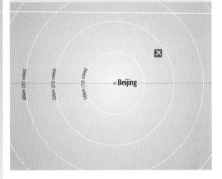

48km (30 miles)    32km (20 miles)    16km (10 miles)    ● Beijing

### ARRIVING AT CAPITAL AIRPORT

The airport (www.bcia.com.cn) is modern and efficient with cafés and curio shops. Be sure to arrive at least two hours in advance when departing; huge Japanese or Chinese tourist groups can clog up the check-in and customs and immigration desks. The rate of airport departure tax is 90 yuan.

The taxi fare into the city is around 100 yuan and cabs are metered—don't try to haggle. The journey takes around 30 minutes, depending on the amount of traffic (it could take as long as an hour at the busiest times). Taxi driving is considered safe but not as safe as in London and New York since many new drivers are taking to the roads. Airport-City's shuttle buses run every 15 minutes (less frequently at night), 24 hours a day, between the airport and the city. The fare is 16 yuan, and the journey takes around 30 minutes. Pick up shuttle buses from the China Aviation Building; drop-offs are outside the airport international terminal. Four other shuttle services (lines) make stops along the way near big hotels and subway stations. These run every 10–30 minutes depending on

the route, from 7am until the last flight (Xidan route). Journey times to the city depend on the number of stops and traffic, but generally you need to reckon at least an hour. Buy tickets from the airport information desk, where a route leaflet is available, or from the sales point by the buses.

The Beijing Airport Express fast rail link connecting Capital Airport with downtown Beijing is under construction and due to open in time for the 2008 Olympics. The driverless trains will run on a 17-mile (27km) track and serve the two existing terminals and Terminal 3 (currently under construction).

### ARRIVING BY TRAIN
There are five rail stations in Beijing. West Railway Station at Lianhuachi handles routes to and from the south and west, including Hong Kong (journey time 28 hours). Other international trains, including the Trans-Siberian Express, arrive at Beijing Zhan station. The remaining three stations handle only domestic services. Remember to retain your ticket until you are out of the terminal. The city's main railway stations are large, busy and complicated. They are invariably surrounded by large crowds of people looking for or waiting for work, and by individuals who hope to hustle arriving foreigners. Try to ensure that you are not overburdened with luggage and can make your way quickly and smoothly to the taxi stands outside (ignoring touts who offer you a taxi on the way). Getting to nearby metro stations or bus stops with a lot of luggage, or with small children in tow, is sure to be far more stressful than lining up for a taxi.

### ARRIVING BY BUS
There are no international bus routes, but the four main stations—Dongzhimen, Haihutun, Yongdingmen and Qianmen—are served by buses from different parts of the country.

# Getting Around

## MAPS

Some hotel stores sell a Chinese/English city map that shows all bus routes, but these are rarely (if ever) up-to-date—even the latest editions are likely to lag a year or two behind the reality on the ground. The good news is that although the Beijing that ordinary Beijingers live in is changing so fast, the attractions that most visitors want to see mostly stay put.

## RETURN ADDRESS

Always carry with you a card or handwritten note in Chinese stating your hotel name and address, and perhaps even directions for how to get there if it is not likely to be well known or in an easily identifiable location. This will be particularly useful for taxi drivers—but might also come in handy should you be involved in an accident or lose your wallet or handbag. An extension of this precaution would be to carry brief information in Chinese about any chronic medical condition you have or medicines you need to take.

## THE SUBWAY

● The subway runs between 5am and 10.30 or 11pm.

● There are five main lines, an east–west line (Line 1); the main circle line (Line 2); a north–south line (Line 5); an eastern extension to Line 1 (Line 8); and a northern loop line (Line 13). Two new lines will be operational in time for the Olympics in 2008.

● Newer trains have air-conditioning, double-glazing and heating.

● Station names are in English on the platforms and an announcement in English is made on the train as it approaches the station.

● Buy tickets inside the station from cash desks and show them to the clerk at the top of the subway staircase. Travel on Lines 1 and 2 costs a flat 3 yuan.

● The new Beijing Municipal Administration and Communications Card, a monthly smart card known as the Yikatong (one-card pass), can be used on the subway, buses and some taxis. A subway-only pass costs 60 yuan, with a refundable 20 yuan deposit. Cards can be bought at outlets such as post offices and topped up.

## TAXIS

● Taxis are inexpensive and plentiful. The standard fare is 2 or 3 yuan per km after the first 3 miles (5km), with a minimum charge of 10 yuan during the day and 13 yuan after 11pm.

● The least expensive taxis are small, uncomfortable yellow vans. Stick with regular small-car taxis.

● Always ask someone at your hotel to write down your destination in Chinese, and show this to the driver before setting off. Ask your hotel doorman to confirm that the taxi driver knows where you are going.

● Taxis can be hailed in the street and also wait at stands outside the airport, stations and major tourist attractions. A "For Hire" sign is illuminated when the meter is off.

● Make sure the meter is switched on at the

start of the journey, and get a receipt when you get out so you can trace the taxi if you accidentally leave something behind.

● Tipping is not the norm.
● The biggest taxi company in Beijing is the Capital Taxi Co. (☎ 6406 5088).

## BUSES

● Beijing has a huge bus network.
● There is a confusing array of vehicles: red and white, blue and white, trolley buses, double-decker buses and private minibuses that carry the same number as the bus route they follow. On minibuses you can always get a seat, and the vehicle will stop anywhere along the route.
● Public buses are often horrendously crowded, particularly at peak times.
● Bus stop signs are in Chinese although bus numbers and times of operation are displayed, and start and end destinations are in pinyin.
● Older buses cost a flat 1 yuan for any journey and have a box by the driver for the exact fare. Air-conditioned buses cost more, the price dependent on the distance. A conductor usually collects the fare, but buses are often so crowded that you have difficulty seeing him.
● The largest bus operator is the Beijing Bus Company (☎ 6396 0088).

## BICYCLES

● Major roads have dedicated cycle lanes. They teem with cyclists each morning and late afternoon—Beijing has around 10 million bicycles.
● Areas such as the *hutongs* and paths alongside rivers are good places to go exploring on two wheels.
● Beijing Kingdom Bicycle Rentals Co. (☎ 8140 0738; www.bicyclekingdom.com) rent bicycles by the day or longer. A fixed-gear bike or a folding bike (which can be taken on the subway) costs 100 yuan for one day, a mountain bike up to 200 yuan (in both cases, the per day rate decreases the more days you rent for). Rental includes a lock, as bicycle theft is a big problem in Beijing.

### TAXI TRIALS

It's asking for trouble to step into one of the illegal taxis that operate from the airports, rail stations and other locations around town. You are certain to be vastly overcharged and can face aggression if you try to resist paying. Never accept an offer from someone who approaches you for a taxi. There are plenty of legal taxis, which can be hailed in the street or at an official taxi stand. They have a "Taxi" sign on the roof that illuminates at night and inside they have a prominently displayed meter and driver permit with photograph.

### CAR RENTAL

● You can rent a vehicle with a driver to get around Beijing. Hotels or local travel agencies will arrange chauffered car rental.
● International firm Avis has a downtown location (☎ 021 6629 1119; www.avischina.com ◎ Daily 8.30–5) through its tie-up with Anji Car Rental and Leasing Co. Drivers will meet clients at the airport, hotel or any other prearranged location. One day's rental for an intermediate car with driver costs 740 yuan.

# Essential Facts

## TOILETS

Hotels, shopping malls, modern department stores and better restaurants have Western-style toilets. Elsewhere expect hole-in-the-ground toilets and standards of cleanliness that are not always good.

## MONEY

RMB (Renminbi) is the currency of China. The basic unit is the yuan (pronounced "kuai"), which is made up of 10 jiao (pronounced "mao"), each of which is again divided into 10 fen. There are notes for 1, 2, 5, 10, 20, 50 and 100 yuan, and the smaller 1, 2 and 5 jiao. There are also coins for 1, 2 and 5 yuan; 1, 2 and 5 jiao; and 1, 2 and 5 fen.

20 yuan

50 yuan

100 yuan

## ELECTRICITY
● The supply is 220 volts, 50 cycles AC current. Sockets come in a variety of sizes and types. Big hotels can supply adaptors, but it is best to bring your own.

## ETIQUETTE
● Confrontation or a public display of anger is counterproductive.
● Other public displays of strong emotion are not advisable.

## MEDICAL TREATMENT
● Better hotels have their own medical services. Clinics with English-speaking staff include:
● Hong Kong International Medical Clinic ☒ Swissotel (Hong Kong Macau Center), 2 Chaoyangmenbei Dajie, Chaoyang District ☎ 6501 4260 (24hr: 6553 2288 ext. 2346)
● International Medical Center ☒ Lufthansa Center, Regus Office Building, Room 106, 50 Liangmaqiao Lu, Chaoyang District ☎ 6465 1561
● Sino-Japanese Friendship Hospital ☒ Yinghua Donglu, Hepingli Beikou ☎ 6422 1122 ext. 3411

## MEDICINES
● Stores in top-class hotels often sell simple medicines—most notably the Watsons store at the Holiday Inn Lido (outside the city center, toward the airport). Some bigger supermarkets, like those in the Lufthansa Center and the China World Trade Shopping Center, are also worth trying. The International Medical Center has a pharmacy.

## MONEY MATTERS
● Most major credit cards are accepted at hotels, and at an increasing number of smarter restaurants and stores.
● Traveler's checks (in dollars) are safer than cash and attract a better exchange rate. They can be cashed at the Bank of China and at bureaux de change.

● If prices are not displayed, polite bargaining is probably expected.

## OPENING HOURS
● Banks and offices: Mon–Fri 9–5.
● Stores: Generally 9–6, often later.

## POST
● The easiest way to send letters and postcards is from your hotel.
● Sending packages is time-consuming and often frustrating since printed matter has to be wrapped by postal officials. Leave parcels open because they must be inspected at the post office.
● Smaller packages can be sent from most post offices. Larger parcels need to go from the main post office: the International Post Office (✉ Jianguomenwai Dajie ☎ 6512 8120).

## SENSIBLE PRECAUTIONS
● Beijing is generally very safe.
● Pickpockets operate in crowded places like rail stations and buses; secure all belongings.
● Leave money and important documents in your hotel room safe or safety-deposit box.
● Always keep traveler's checks separate from your record of their numbers, and note the emergency contact number in case of loss.
● Bring a photocopy of your passport and visa in case of theft.

## TELEPHONES
● Local calls cost about 50 jiao, and hotels usually only charge a nominal mark-up.
● The easiest and least expensive way to make an international call is to use a card telephone in a hotel. Cards come in denominations of 100 yuan and may be purchased from hotel shops and hotel business centers.
● Use business centers in hotels to send faxes and emails. You do not have to be a guest.

## TIPPING
● Tipping is not expected, except for guides.

### EMERGENCY PHONE NUMBERS
● Police 110. Ambulance 120. Fire 119 (Chinese only).

### TOURIST OFFICES
There is no tourist information office but the Beijing Tourism Administration operates a tourist hotline and website: ☎ 6513 0828; www.bjta.gov.cn

### EMBASSIES AND CONSULATES
● **Australia** ✉ 21 Dongzhimenwai Dajie ☎ 5140 4111
● **Canada** ✉ 19 Dongzhimenwai Dajie ☎ 6532 3536
● **France** ✉ 3 Dongsanjie, Sanlitun ☎ 8532 8080
● **Germany** ✉ 17 Dongzhimenwai Dajie ☎ 6532 2161
● **Ireland** ✉ 3 Ritan Donglu ☎ 6532 2914
● **New Zealand** ✉ 1 Ritan Dong'erjie, Jianguomenwai Dajie ☎ 6532 2731
● **UK** ✉ 11 Guanghua Lu, Jianguomenwai Dajie ☎ 5192 4000; Visa and consular services ✉ 21st floor, North Tower, Kerry Centre, 1 Guanghua Lu ☎ 8529 6600
● **USA** ✉ 3 Xiushui Beijie, Jianguomenwai Dajie ☎ 6532 3831 ext. 209

# Language

In general, the better the hotel the better the standard of English spoken and understood. On the street, you cannot rely on communicating in any language other than Chinese. Although many people know some English, it is useful (as well as courteous) to know some basic spoken Chinese. The modern phonetic romanized form of Chinese is called "pinyin." It is largely pronounced as written, but note the following:

a as in car
c as in bits as an initial consonant
e as in her
i as in feet unless preceded by c, ch, r, s, sh, z, sh, when it
    becomes er as in her
j as in gin
o as in ford
q like the ch in chin
s as in simple
u as in oo in cool
w as in wade, though pronounced by some as v
x like the sh in sheep but with the s given greater emphasis
y as in yoyo
z as ds in lids; zh as j in jam

| BASIC VOCABULARY | |
|---|---|
| hello | ni hao |
| please | qing |
| thank you | xiexie |
| goodbye | zai jian |
| My surname is... | Wo xing... |
| I am from... | Who shi...laide |
| yes | shi |
| no | bu shi |
| I don't understand | bu dong |
| Do you understand? | Dong ma? |
| when? | shenme shi hou? |
| where? | nar? |
| telephone | dianhua |
| police | jingcha |
| toilet | ce suo |
| excuse me | dui bu qi |
| time | shijian |
| doctor | yi sheng |
| hospital | yiyuan |
| pharmacy | yaodian |

| NUMBERS | |
|---|---|
| 0 | ling |
| 1 | yi, yao |
| 2 | er, liang |
| 3 | san |
| 4 | si |
| 5 | wu |
| 6 | liu |
| 7 | qi |
| 8 | ba |
| 9 | jiu |
| 10 | shi |
| 11 | shiyi |
| 12 | shier |
| 20 | ershi |
| 21 | ershiyi |
| 100 | yibai |
| 200 | erbai |
| 1,000 | yiqian |

## GETTING AROUND

| | |
|---|---|
| where is...? | ...zai nali? |
| taxi | chuzu che |
| airport | fei ji chang |
| train | huoche |
| bus | gong gong qi che |
| bicycle | xi xing che |
| ticket | piao |
| turn right | you zhuan |
| turn left | zuo zhuan |
| I'm lost | Wo milule |
| hotel | fandian |
| room | fang jian |
| post office | youju |
| bank | yin hang |

## SHOPPING

| | |
|---|---|
| how much? | Duo shao qian? |
| too expensive | tai gui le |
| a little cheaper | pian yi dian ba |
| gift | li wu |
| credit card | xin yong ka |
| postcards | ming xin pian |
| stamps | you piao |
| antique | guwu |
| silk | sichou |
| rice | mifan |
| beer | pijiu |
| coffee | ka fei |

# Timeline

### "OLD BUDDHA"

Empress Dowager Cixi (1834–1908) first entered the Forbidden City as one of many concubines to a Manchu emperor. When he died in 1861, she became regent to their infant son. From then until her death, she was the effective ruler of China—a deeply conservative figure renowned for, among other things, releasing 10,000 caged birds each year on her birthday and spending lavishly on herself. She acquired the nickname Old Buddha, and following her son's death, chose her nephew as emperor. When he tried to introduce reforms, she had him confined to the palace as a virtual prisoner. The day before she died, she successfully organized his murder.

*The Gate of Supreme Harmony; the Great Wall; Chairman Mao; Soong Qing-Ling; the national emblem of the People's Republic of China (left to right)*

$700BC$ Mongols, Koreans and local Chinese trade on the site that is now Beijing.

$AD1215$ Mongol warrior Genghis Khan captures Youzhou (Tranquil City) and his grandson Kublai establishes the renamed Dadu (Great Capital), the site of the future capital, Beijing.

$1368$ The second Ming emperor becomes the great architect of Beijing, building the Forbidden City.

$1644$ The Qing dynasty expands the capital over the next century and builds the great Summer Palace.

$1860$ Anglo-French troops attack Beijing and burn the Summer Palace during the Opium Wars. In 1884, Dowager Empress Cixi commissions a new Summer Palace. Sealed within the Forbidden City, she is oblivious to the poverty in the country.

$1911$ Occupation by successive waves of foreign troops weakens the imperial order. The Nationalist Party establishes the Republic of China.

$1928$ Chiang Kai Shek controls Beijing until the city falls to Japan in 1937. After 1945, the civil war that began in 1927 resumes between Chiang and Mao Zedong's Communists.

*1949* The victorious Mao announces the People's Republic of China, and the remnants of Chiang's Nationalists flee to Taiwan. Soviet experts help rebuild large parts of Beijing.

*1966* Mao launches his Cultural Revolution in Beijing, a master move in a power struggle in the Communist Party. Red Guards wave their little red books, and schools close for a decade.

*1976* Mao dies, and Deng Xiaoping takes power. Westerners are admitted into China, and foreign investment is allowed in special economic zones.

*1989* Students mass in Tian'anmen Square to demand political liberalization. The government calls in the army. Hundreds—possibly thousands—are killed.

*1997* Return of Hong Kong to Chinese rule.

*2001* China enters the World Trade Organization, and Beijing wins the bid to host the 2008 Olympics. An ambitious program of building projects gets under way.

*2004* China's Olympic athletes return from the Athens Games with 63 medals (including 32 golds) and are congratulated by President Hu Jintao in the Great Hall of the People.

*2008* The 2008 Summer Olympic Games are held in Beijing.

### MAO ZEDONG

The son of a wealthy farmer in Hunan province, Mao adapted Marxism to suit rural China. When his fellow Communists were threatened by Chiang Kai Shek, he organized the famous year-long, 5,890-mile (9,500km) Long March across 18 mountain ranges and 24 rivers to escape capture. After he proclaimed the People's Republic of China in 1949, his policies dominated Chinese life until 1976. Despite official acknowledgment that Mao made some mistakes–the exact percentage is a matter of arcane disputation–he remains a deeply revered figure among older Chinese, and his influence continues to be felt.

# Index

INDEX

**INDEX**

# Beijing's
## 25 Best

**WRITTEN BY** Sean Sheehan
**ADDITIONAL WRITING BY** George McDonald
**DESIGN CONCEPT AND DESIGN WORK** Kate Harling
**COVER DESIGN** Tigist Getachew
**INDEXER** Marie Lorimer
**IMAGE RETOUCHING AND REPRO** Michael Moody, Sarah Montgomery and Matt Swann
**REVIEWING EDITOR** Jacinta O'Halloran
**EDITOR** Marie-Claire Jefferies
**SERIES EDITOR** Paul Mitchell

Fodor's is a registered trademark of Random House, Inc.
Published in the United Kingdom by AA Publishing

**ISBN 978-1-4000-1874-1**

**FIFTH EDITION**

**IMPORTANT TIP**
Time inevitably brings changes, so always confirm prices, travel facts, and other perishable information when it matters. Although Fodor's cannot accept responsibility for errors, you can use this guide in the confidence that we have taken every care to ensure its accuracy.

**SPECIAL SALES**
This book is available for special discounts for bulk purchases for sales promotions or premiums. Special editions, including personalized covers, excerpts of existing books, and corporate imprints, can be created in large quantities for special needs. For more information, write to Special Markets/Premium Sales, 1745 Broadway, MD 6–2, New York, NY 10019 or email specialmarkets@randomhouse.com.

Colour separation by Keenes
Printed and bound by Leo, China
10 9 8 7 6 5 4 3 2 1

A03144
Maps in this title produced from mapping © MAIRDUMONT / Falk Verlag 2007
Transport map © Communicarta Ltd, UK

The Automobile Association wishes to thank the following photographers and organisations for their assistance in the preparation of this book.

Abbreviations for the picture credits are as follows – (t) top; (b) bottom; (l) left; (r) right; (c) centre; (b/g) background; (AA) AA World Travel Library

1 AA/A Mockford & N Bonetti; 2-18t AA/A Mockford & N Bonetti; 4l AA/A Mockford & N Bonetti; 5c AA/A Mockford & N Bonetti; 6cl AA/A Mockford & N Bonetti; 6c AA/A Mockford & N Bonetti; 6r AA/A Mockford & N Bonetti; 6bl AA/A Mockford & N Bonetti; 6bc AA/A Mockford & N Bonetti; 6br Digitalvision; 7cl AA/A Mockford & N Bonetti; 7cr AA/A Mockford & N Bonetti; 7bl AA/A Mockford & N Bonetti; 7bc AA/A Mockford & N Bonetti; 7br AA/A Mockford & N Bonetti; 10tr AA/A Mockford & N Bonetti; 10cr AA/A Mockford & N Bonetti; 10/11c AA/A Mockford & N Bonetti; 10/11b AA/A Mockford & N Bonetti; 11tl AA/A Mockford & N Bonetti; 11cl Anna Mockford and Nick Bonetti; 12b AA/A Mockford & N Bonetti; 13tl AA/A Mockford & N Bonetti; 13tcl AA/A Mockford & N Bonetti; 13cl AA/A Mockford & N Bonetti; 13bl AA/A Mockford & N Bonetti; 14tr AA/A Mockford & N Bonetti; 14tcr AA/A Mockford & N Bonetti; 14cr AA/A Mockford & N Bonetti; 14br AA/A Mockford & N Bonetti; 15b AA/A Mockford & N Bonetti; 16tr AA/A Mockford & N Bonetti; 16cr AA/A Mockford & N Bonetti; 16br Digitalvision; 17tl AA/A Mockford & N Bonetti; 17cl AA/A Mockford & N Bonetti; 17cl AA/A Mockford & N Bonetti; 17bl AA/A Mockford & N Bonetti; 18tr AA/G Clements; 18cr AA/A Mockford & N Bonetti; 18cr AA/A Kouprianoff; 18br AA/I Morejohn; 19t AA/A Mockford & N Bonetti; 19ct AA/A Mockford & N Bonetti; 19c AA/A Mockford & N Bonetti; 19cb AA/A Mockford & N Bonetti; 19b AA/A Mockford & N Bonetti; 20-21 AA/A Mockford & N Bonetti; 24 AA/A Mockford & N Bonetti; 25l AA/A Mockford & N Bonetti; 25c AA/A Mockford & N Bonetti; 25r AA/A Mockford & N Bonetti; 26l AA/A Mockford & N Bonetti; 26tr AA/A Mockford & N Bonetti; 26cr AA/A Mockford & N Bonetti; 27t AA/G Clements; 27cl AA/G Clements; 27cr AA/G Clements; 28tl AA/A Mockford & N Bonetti; 28cl AA/A Mockford & N Bonetti; 28cc AA/G Clements; 28/29tc AA/G Clements; 28/29c AA/G Clements; 29r AA/A Mockford & N Bonetti; 30l AA/G Clements; 30tr AA/G Clements; 30cr AA/G Clements; 31t AA/G Clements; 31cl AA/G Clements; 31cr AA/G Clements; 32t AA/A Mockford & N Bonetti; 32cl AA/A Mockford & N Bonetti; 32c AA/G Clements; 32cr AA/A Mockford & N Bonetti; 33 AA/A Mockford & N Bonetti; 34l AA/A Mockford & N Bonetti; 34c AA/A Mockford & N Bonetti; 35r AA/A Mockford & N Bonetti; 36-37t AA/A Mockford & N Bonetti; 36b AA/A Mockford & N Bonetti; 37b AA/G Clements; 38t AA/A Mockford & N Bonetti; 39 AA/A Mockford & N Bonetti; 43l AA/G Clements; 43r AA/A Mockford & N Bonetti; 44l AA/A Mockford & N Bonetti; 44r AA/A Mockford & N Bonetti; 45l AA/A Mockford & N Bonetti; 45c AA/G Clements; 45r AA/A Mockford & N Bonetti; 46 AA/G Clements; 47 AA/G Clements; 48 AA/A Mockford & N Bonetti; 49l AA/A Mockford & N Bonetti; 49c AA/A Mockford & N Bonetti; 49r AA/A Mockford & N Bonetti; 50t AA/A Mockford & N Bonetti; 50cl Anna Mockford and Nick Bonetti; 50cr AA/A Mockford & N Bonetti; 51 AA/A Mockford & N Bonetti; 52l AA/A Mockford & N Bonetti; 52tr AA/A Mockford & N Bonetti; 52cr AA/A Mockford & N Bonetti; 53t AA/A Mockford & N Bonetti; 53cl AA/A Mockford & N Bonetti; 53cr AA/A Mockford & N Bonetti; 54t-56t AA/A Mockford & N Bonetti; 54bl AA/G Clements; 54br AA/G Clements; 55bl AA/A Mockford & N Bonetti; 55br AA/G Clements; 56bl AA/A Kouprianoff; 56br AA/A Mockford & N Bonetti; 57 AA/A Mockford & N Bonetti; 58-59t AA/A Mockford & N Bonetti; 60t AA/A Mockford & N Bonetti; 61-62t AA/A Mockford & N Bonetti; 63 AA/A Mockford & N Bonetti; 66l AA/A Mockford & N Bonetti; 66r AA/A Mockford & N Bonetti; 67 Agence Images/Alamy; 68l AA/A Kouprianoff; 68tr AA/A Mockford & N Bonetti; 68cr AA/A Mockford & N Bonetti; 69t AA/A Mockford & N Bonetti; 69cl AA/A Mockford & N Bonetti; 69c AA/A Mockford & N Bonetti; 69cr AA/A Mockford & N Bonetti; 70tl AA/A Mockford & N Bonetti; 70cl AA/A Mockford & N Bonetti; 70cc AA/G Clements; 71tl AA/A Mockford & N Bonetti; 71r AA/G Clements; 71cl AA/G Clements; 71cc AA/A Mockford & N Bonetti; 72 AA/A Mockford & N Bonetti; 73 AA/A Mockford & N Bonetti; 74-75t AA/A Mockford & N Bonetti; 76 AA/A Mockford & N Bonetti; 77 AA/A Mockford & N Bonetti; 80l AA/A Mockford & N Bonetti; 80tr AA/G Clements; 80cr AA/A Kouprianoff; 81t AA/I Morejohn; 81cl AA/A Mockford & N Bonetti; 81cr AA/A Mockford & N Bonetti; 82l AA/A Mockford & N Bonetti; 82/83t AA/A Mockford & N Bonetti; 82cr AA/A Mockford & N Bonetti; 83r AA/A Mockford & N Bonetti; 83c AA/A Mockford & N Bonetti; 84-85t AA/A Mockford & N Bonetti; 84bl AA/A Mockford & N Bonetti; 84br AA/A Mockford & N Bonetti; 85bl AA/A Mockford & N Bonetti; 85br AA/A Mockford & N Bonetti; 86 AA/A Mockford & N Bonetti; 87 AA/A Mockford & N Bonetti; 88 AA/A Mockford & N Bonetti; 89-90t AA/A Mockford & N Bonetti; 91 AA/A Mockford & N Bonetti; 94l AA/A Mockford & N Bonetti; 94c AA/A Mockford & N Bonetti; 94r AA/A Mockford & N Bonetti; 95l AA/G Clements; 95c AA/G Clements; 95r AA/G Clements; 96l AA/A Mockford & N Bonetti; 96r AA/A Mockford & N Bonetti; 97 AA/A Mockford & N Bonetti; 98l AA/I Morejohn; 98/99 AA/A Kouprianoff; 100l AA/A Mockford & N Bonetti; 100tr AA/A Mockford & N Bonetti; 100cr AA/A Mockford & N Bonetti; 101t AA/A Mockford & N Bonetti; 101cl AA/A Mockford & N Bonetti; 101cr AA/A Mockford & N Bonetti; 102l AA/G Clements; 102c AA/G Clements; 102r AA/G Clements; 103t AA/A Mockford & N Bonetti; 103b AA/A Mockford & N Bonetti; 103r Víctor Guisado; 104 Liu Xiaoyang/Alamy; 105t Panorama Media (Beijing) Ltd/Alamy; 106t Panorama Media (Beijing) Ltd/Alamy; 107 AA/A Mockford & N Bonetti; 108-112t AA/C Sawyer; 108tr AA/A Mockford & N Bonetti; 108cr AA/A Mockford & N Bonetti; 108cr AA/A Mockford & N Bonetti; 108br AA/A Mockford & N Bonetti; 113 AA/A Mockford & N Bonetti; 114-125t AA/A Mockford & N Bonetti; 115br AA/A Mockford & N Bonetti; 120 MRI Bankers Guide to Foreign Currency, Houston, USA; 123tr AA/A Mockford & N Bonetti; 123cr AA/A Mockford & N Bonetti; 123cr AA/A Mockford & N Bonetti; 123b AA/A Mockford & N Bonetti; 124bl AA/G Clements; 124bc AA/A Mockford & N Bonetti; 124/125c AA/G Clements; 125bc AA/A Mockford & N Bonetti; 125br AA/A Mockford & N Bonetti

Every effort has been made to trace the copyright holders, and we apologise in advance for any unintentional omissions or errors. We would be pleased to apply any corrections in any following edition of this publication.